Time For Change

Other books by Anne J. Townsend

Families without Pretending
Marriage without Pretending
Missionary without Pretending
Prayer without Pretending
Suffering without Pretending
Faun and the naughtiest pig
Together for God

Time For Change

How To Grow With Your Teenagers

Anne J. Townsend

Marshalls

Dedication

For my husband, John.

Whose security as a person and whose unshakeable faith in God has helped us as a family to weather life's storms, and to enjoy the calms in-between.

Marshalls Paperbacks
Marshall Morgan & Scott

1 Bath Street, London EC1V 9LB

Copyright © Anne J. Townsend 1982
First published by Marshall Morgan & Scott 1982

ISBN 0 551 00971 3
Printed in Great Britain by
Hunt Barnard Printing Ltd., Aylesbury, Bucks.

Contents

Introduction   **11**

One: A time of change   **13**
     Understanding ourselves
     Uncharted territory
     Changing ways
     Semi-strangers
     Rapid developments
     Deceptive signs
     Bewildering changes
     Play it cool

Two: Facing the differences   **22**
     Painful questions
     Under the microscope
     Constant criticism
     Saying 'sorry'
     Experiencing Jesus for himself
     Trailing along to church
     Time alone
     Teen culture
     Feelings
     Letting go
     Of infinite value

Three: The importance of independence   **31**
     Parents with problems
     The right friends
     Keeping your distance
     Handling yourself
     Decision-making

His territory
Knowing the law
Making a change

Four: Conformity and non-conformity   41
Teenage gear
Not your taste
Gangs and groups
Conflicting views
Divided loyalties
Coping with conflict
What does God want?
Beneath the surface

Five: The value of disagreement   52
Over-reaction
Other families
Sharing your failure
Family life with God
Rules and regulations
Non-stop music
Sexual standards
Face reality together

Six: Parents in mid-life crisis   62
Take yourself in hand
Men and dads
Women and mums
Reinforcing your marriage
Falling in love at forty
Cold war marriages
Your vulnerability
Church commitments
Accepting your failures

Seven: What is home?   71
Unconditional love
Open house
Family finances
Depending on God
Making allowances

Tight budgets
Giving to God
Running the home

Eight: Sex in a secular society   80
Pressures of permissiveness
Parents — your crucial role
Government concern
Appalling facts
Teach teenagers 'no'
Giving support
What sex is all about
Embarrassment about sex
Spotlight on you

Nine: Learning to love   89
Sexual differences
Sleeping together
Marriage expectations
Deep relationships
Women today
Testing friendships
First love

Ten: Guilty feelings about sexuality   97
'Unforgiveable' sins
Masturbation
Fantasies
Homosexual leanings
Unnecessary guilt
Guilt and sexuality

Eleven: Your teenager's future   106
Your motives
What price academic success?
Parental pressure
Your child's character
In his majesty's service
Hearing God's call
People before paper

Twelve: Support through school   114
    Jekyll and Hyde
    Disrupting difficulties
    Responses to stress
    Going to meetings
    Responsible actions

Thirteen: Coping with exams   122
    Sorting out priorities
    The value of school trips
    Preparing for exams
    'Exam nerves'
    Parents' provision

Fourteen: Leaving school   130
    A final fling of youth
    Facing exam results
    Decisions and procedure
    Assessing his qualities
    A first job
    Real money
    Pressures from advertising
    Job-hunting in a depressed market

Fifteen: Coming from a Christian home   139
    Your child and Christianity
    Death and suffering
    Points of conversion
    Fellowship at school
    True friendships

Sixteen: Drink and drug abuse   147
    Teenage alcoholism
    The significance of alcohol
    Alcohol abuse
    Parental influence
    The remedy
    Giving up drink
    The drug scene
    Getting help

Seventeen: When to seek help 155
Physical problems
Warning signs
Slimming and starving
Anorexia nervosa
Doing your best

Introduction

This book is for parents of teenagers, and since British culture is inconsistent, it is written for Christian parents who regard themselves as 'middle class'.

Attitudes to teenagers vary throughout the different levels of our society, as do standards and values. Therefore what applies at one level does not necessarily fit in with the culture of other levels. One level is not right and another wrong — they are different. And it is this difference which means that this book is for middle class parents.

This book is about girls as well as boys — the use of 'he' is for convenience and brevity only.

I hope you will find this book as helpful to read as I have found it to write.

Anne Townsend
November 1981

1: A time of change

My son looked down at me. 'All right little mother,' his face creased into a teasing smile, 'since you asked me to do it, and didn't tell me to, I'll do it for you. . .'

Those words made me realise that, at fifteen, my youngest child was no longer the little boy I sometimes assumed him to be. Not only was he taller than my five feet four but he was also growing into a responsible adult in his own right. And if that was true for him, then how much more for my other two children: one approaching her twenties and the other in his sixth form at school.

Like many parents I was in danger of not seeing the obvious — that my children could hardly be called that any more. They were heading for adulthood at an alarming rate. And somewhere I had been left on the sidelines, and almost overlooked what was going on in my own family. I had almost missed some of the most important years of my children's lives.

If I am honest, I have to admit that these were years I wouldn't have minded missing. Some parents derive pleasure from their children's teenage years, but I found much of this time bewildering and hurtful. In sharing with other parents I find that I am not alone in this. And we admit to one another that the main reason we have not been able to helpfully understand our children's formative teenage years is because we have not understood what was happening inside ourselves, let alone what was going on inside our children.

Understanding ourselves

The fact that my children were in their teens hit me hard last winter. As I went out for a morning's shopping in the January sales, I knew I was tired after all the work involved in a family Christmas. Tired as I was, I re-assured myself that this was the reason I felt, and looked, old. 'A new dress,' I tried to convince myself, 'a new hair style and new lipstick and then you'll be your old self again. . .' My optimism was misplaced. I stood alone in the changing room of a large department store; a pile of glamorous dresses discarded on the chair. The harsh neon light hit my face, and I shut my eyes to blot out the reflection thrown at me by the mirror. I hadn't examined my face for so long or so carefully for years. There I was with what seemed to me to be a deep ravine bisecting my forehead, and creases looking like ugly crow's feet spreading out from my eyes. One of my friends had once commented: 'Those are the lines of experience . . . when I look at you I know what you have been through and what caused each one of those lines'. At that moment, in that shop, I longed for the fresh unlined face that had been mine twenty years earlier, before my children were born. The pile of dis-carded dresses deflated my self-confidence further, and I could almost hear my daughter's advice, 'Don't try wearing that sort of style, Mum, it really doesn't suit you. . .' Words that were tactful and loving but which told me I was getting old; too old to wear the sort of clothes a younger person could wear; and my problem was that I did not feel as old as my teenagers made me out to be.

I combed the rails of dresses again. Yes, there it was! The familiar style that I knew I could wear anywhere at any time; and it would hide my deficient waistline and the middle-aged spread that I was convinced was not there but which my sons were equally insistent was all too visible. There was nothing wrong with the dress I bought. I knew that any other day I would have selected it from choice and liked it. In a flash of insight, as I went down in the store lift, I realised why I had suddenly disliked my favourite style. I wanted to be like my daughter. I wanted to be young, slim and beautiful like her. I longed to lose my tiring middle-aged shape, and to be like her again. It was hard to admit the truth that, in a peculiar way, I was jealous of my daughter's youth and freshness. I felt old and worn-out. The interesting thing was that once I had admitted that I had a problem with myself I was able to tackle it, and work at boosting my sagging self-esteem.

Being the parent of a teenager entails more than trying to understand the changes your child is weathering. It also involves understanding the changes through which you, the parents, happen to be passing at the same time; as you face mid-life changes with possible 'mid-life crises'. That is why parents of teenagers need to understand themselves as well as what is happening to their teenagers.

Uncharted territory

One problem in being a parent is that you have no first-hand experience. None of us quite know if we're getting it right or not, we cannot look it up in a book. Although there are stacks of books on rearing your baby, disciplining your toddler, learning to read, there are remarkably few books that tell you how to be good parents to your teenagers. By the time we have the end results to look at to assess the validity of our methods, it's too late to change them. Yet we don't listen to our parents' advice. We dismiss them with: 'What can they possibly know about it. Life for young people today is totally different from what it was when we were young. The old don't have anything to say that's relevant or worth listening to. . .'

So, you and I, the parents of teenagers may feel as if we are setting sail on an uncharted sea, bereft of any nice little pocket guides that guarantee success.

Changing ways

While your child is still under ten, he accepts you as you are. He probably doesn't understand you as a person because he isn't capable of doing so, nor has he any need to at this stage of life. You will probably have found that he tends to unquestioningly accept what you do, and the fact that you have the authority to tell him what to do and what not to do. He does not expect anything different. If he compares you with other parents then it is likely to be in the uncritical fashion of, 'Alice is allowed to watch the midnight movie on tv . . . can't I watch it too?' If you reply: 'No!' then he may moan but that is the end of it. With teenagers you enter an era where all that is changed. Your 'no' will be followed by a long, ethical and probing debate, or straight refusal. Again, when your child reaches ten or eleven you may find that you are excluded from some of his activities. This is a subtle change heralding his first steps into the independence that he will attain as an adult. You may feel slighted, rejected, excluded or unwanted for the first time in your child's life. If this happens to you then try to forget about yourself and rejoice in the fact that your child is developing as a normal child ought to.

Semi-strangers

Realizing what is happening to you can dawn gradually or strike suddenly. Gazing at your child one morning at breakfast, you may suddenly think: 'Who's this stranger? Where's the person I tucked up in bed last night. . . I don't know this half-child, half-adult who is sitting there pontificating about a subject I didn't know he had heard about. . .' That child, who once had a warm, close relationship with you now seems to have turned into a semi-stranger. You used to know his mind, but now his thoughts are semi-secret and he doesn't want to discuss too much, in too much depth, with you.

If you are like me, then you will assume that there is some huge breakdown in communication between you and your teenager. You will think that you have done something to offend; that you have broken some law governing good parent-teenage relationships. Forget it! Most teenagers prefer to keep their developing thoughts and ideas to themselves. And the chattering nine year old who used to share confidences with you, now needs someone else to try his thoughts out on. So, don't decide you are a hopeless parent when your teenager is simply behaving in a perfectly normal teenage way.

Rapid developments

With the onset of adolescence rapid changes take place in your child's body. Developing sex glands release chemicals into the blood stream; and these affect different organs, tissues and the central nervous system. You can watch obvious physical changes taking place. Your daughter's breasts begin to swell and to develop, fat is laid down in different parts of her body giving her feminine curves, and her menstrual cycle starts and gradually develops with monthly regularity. And as your son enters adolescence you may notice that his testicles and penis enlarge, his voice breaks and hair develops on his face and body. It is also important that you are aware of the profound psychological changes that take place. Ignore these and life will be unnecessarily difficult both for you and for your child. For example, your daughter will be as prone to pre-menstrual tension as her mother is, and it is worth knowing that this sometimes occurs monthly before periods start. If you see that she is getting moody or depressed at the same time every month recognize this as one of the factors heralding her emergence into womanhood. Try to be extra tactful and uncritical if you notice that she is suffering from pre-menstrual tension. Help her to learn to handle herself when she is moody for no apparent reason. Buy or borrow some of the excellent secular books available to help her understand what is going on and why she is reacting as she is.

Deceptive signs

Looking at your child as he starts adult life, you may think: 'He's almost there at last!' But don't heave a sigh of relief too quickly. Looks can be deceptive at this stage. Physical growth does not necessarily mean that mental development has kept up at the same pace. The lad who happens to have shot up in height and whose voice is broken may in fact be less mature emotionally than a boy with a squeaky voice and no sign of a hair on his upper lip. For there is no such thing as an exact average rate for teenage development. Adolescent changes usually begin about the age of ten but as no two children are exactly alike, there is no precise age. You will find that girls usually go through normal teenage developmental stages ahead of boys. But each child is an individual and each develops at the rate that is normal for him. Don't assume there is something wrong with your son if he isn't at the stage your daughter reached at the same age. If you are seriously worried in case your child is either developing too slowly or too fast then go and see your doctor about it. But don't compare your child with other children — it will do little more than cause anxiety both for you and for your child. You cannot mark your teenager's development like easy charts in the best baby books, because teenager's don't develop in the same way that babies do. Your child may develop into adulthood in a slow and steady growth pattern, or he may be the sort of child who grows in fits and starts. You know, the kind of teenager for whom you buy clothes only to find a few weeks later that nothing fits any more, especially shoes!

Today's young are under intense pressure to grow up and enter the adult world as quickly as possible. Yet no one is a fully mature adult at eighteen; nor, come to that, at the age of sixty. Make allowances for your teenager and don't expect too much too soon. And remember that if your child's adolescence perplexes you, then it is far more bewildering and trying for your teenager. He is going through so many changes that it is hard to keep up with himself.

Bewildering changes

Most teenagers go through agonies as they face all the different changes going on in their bodies. It is easy in some families to let this be the current family joke but this is neither a kind nor a loving topic. When your daughter wears her first bra keep quiet about it . . . don't tell everyone.

Your adolescent may well be at his least attractive and may be difficult for you to cope with around the house. Be extra patient at this difficult stage of his life. He knows that he is all arms, legs, knees and elbows, that his face is spotty and his hair tatty, without you reminding him, and he doesn't like it any more than you do. So, don't comment on it. Be tactful in helping him through an unco-ordinated phase of gawky limbs. It helps neither him nor you if you insist on nagging and pointing out the obvious: 'You've knocked over the flowers this morning, the sugar basin this afternoon, the milk this evening . . . what's left!' His despair is greater than yours. Remember that he neither wants to be like this nor chose it. He dislikes this part of growing up.

The phase between being a child and being an adult seems like a twilight zone to some parents and children — a time of conflict, fraught with tensions. Changes occur at such high speed that your teenager has to adapt at a rate greater than any parent can ever appreciate. It is a time for new schools, new friends, new thoughts and new attitudes. In seven years your teenager will be handling more changes than you probably have done in all the rest of your life since you emerged from adolescence yourself. We all find change hard: so spare more than a thought for your teenagers. Maybe your children will be among the few who pass through adolescence with minimal upheavals. If this is so, then be grateful, but don't take this for granted. Most teenagers pass through storms; some are just better at hiding conflicts from parents than others are.

Trying to understand will be further complicated by the confusing range of emotional changes. These are much harder to pinpoint than physical changes. You may think you understand and that everything is clear, then suddenly you find that he has dramatically changed his views or attitudes, and is saying the opposite of what he said before. One moment he may be in seventh heaven and the next in total despair. When your teenager's hormones get going he finds it very difficult to control his emotional reactions. Don't rush off to the doctor for a prescription for tranquillisers for you, or for him! This is one of those difficult stages that has to be worked through; and the hard work is mainly being done by your teenager. So don't feel sorry for yourself, it's worse for him!

Some young people are more affected than others. So, if your teenager is placid and never feels intensely about anything just be grateful, and don't assume his hormone balance is wildly abnormal. No two teenagers are the same!

Play it cool

If your aim is for religion to be central to your life as a family, then you will find this a difficult time for your family to weather together. Your teenager will question your Christian belief. It may even seem as if he has rejected the faith in which you long to see him firmly rooted. On the other hand, he may appear to go overboard with ultra-enthusiasm for Christianity. These are the years when you, as Christian parents, need to play it cool. Don't over-react. Try and be consistent, unshockable and deeply sure of your faith. Hold onto your teenager in prayer and bring him daily to God for him to work in your child's life. This is the time to talk to God about your child more than talking about God to your child. Give your child the breathing space, and the time that he needs to develop spiritually. Give him time to mature as a person before you take seriously any statements he makes for or against Christianity.

If you think that patience is all you need to see your child through the weeks, months or years of intense emotional fluctuation then you are mistaken! You need to be flexible and quick on the uptake. You may need to be like a wall, against which he can bounce the balls of all the different ideas chasing round his mind. Remember that your teenager wants you to remain solid so that he can play off his thoughts and ideas against you, secure in the knowledge that you are one of the unchanging factors in his rapidly changing world, with unshakeable faith and standards. He needs you to be like that. And he wants to feel that you understand what he is saying, and that your ideas are not so rigidly fixed that you cannot see other view points.

In our family my teenagers can look to their father to provide these elements. I am grateful to have a husband who is solid and sure. When we married I knew he would be a good father to our children — it is now, years later, that I see and appreciate the gold that he is to our teenagers by his quiet dependability and unshakeable faith in God.

2: Facing the differences

One of the funniest men I know was not joking when he asked me: 'Please pray for my son.' His brown eyes spelt out his frustration. I had heard similar requests before. I waited for him to continue. 'He just cannot make up his mind what he wants to do. We've sent off for so many different things that it's hard to keep up with him . . . he seems to be definitely going to read maths one day, but by the time we've found out about maths degrees he's changed his mind to something totally different. Now it's archaeology . . .' I nodded in sympathy. My three had never led us quite the same dance but I knew in principle, and to a lesser degree in practise, what he was facing, the constant vacillation, questioning and criticism which all parents of teenagers have to come to terms with.

Painful questions
You may notice that when your child is about twelve years old he begins to develop a sense of self-awareness. This peaks somewhere between the ages of fifteen and seventeen. Until this is fully developed he is not completely awakened as an adult. At the same time, his capacity for abstract thinking and reasoning is developing and he goes through a difficult stage of questioning everything deeply. This may surprise both you and him — you may not have realised that it was latent within him before. And the emergence of a young philosopher can be rather unnerving to an unsuspecting, unexpectant family.

As these aspects of your teenager's personality develop

he begins to ask himself questions that are so potentially painful that he would prefer to avoid them. Questions like: 'What kind of person am I?', 'If anyone knows what I'm really like will I still be loved and accepted, or will I be rejected?' and 'How do I compare with other people — better or worse?' The answers will be coloured by his childhood experiences. If he has grown up in a secure loving environment, then he will find it easier to accept and love the person that he is. Learning to accept and love himself is an important part of growing up. And when I say 'loving himself' I do not mean a selfish love but rather an acceptance of himself as a person designed by God — a person who has flaws that need correcting but one who can accept himself in the same way that he is accepted by God.

Under the microscope

Around the same time, your teenager begins to look at relationships. Studying those around him with an often uncomfortable and painful scrutiny, he compares and contrasts the values he discerns in different relationships, and then makes his own assessments.

He looks carefully at home, school, church and the world, asking age-old questions, as if he was the first ever to query: 'What is life really about?' and 'What is the purpose of me being here in this world?' But he is unlikely to ask you these questions; after all, you are only his parents, and at this stage of life your job is not to give wise philosophical answers — leave that to other people.

You are likely to feel uncomfortable at this stage in your child's development. It is one thing to be under scrutiny from people outside your home who do not know all the hidden quirks that you display there. It is quite another matter to be put under a microscope and dissected by your children who know as much about you as anyone. All your little foibles and inconsistencies have not, you discover, gone unnoticed. Try not to allow yourself to be threatened by this process. After all, if your child needs to learn to accept himself, then he will learn it quickest by seeing you accept yourself . . . and that means accepting yourself with all the foibles that become family jokes. Yes, laugh at yourself where you see that you are rather ridiculous, and let your family laugh both at and with you. If you can do this, then you are well on the way to teaching your teenagers how to accept themselves with, what seems to them, their great deficiencies.

However, not all your teenager's comments should be treated light-heartedly. If you hear it stated of yourself: 'His Christianity is a load of hypocrisy . . . he says one thing in church on Sunday but you should hear what goes on at lunch afterwards. . .' then take those words seriously. God gives us teenagers, I am convinced, to help many of us parents to see ourselves as we are — and to change some of the unlovely and inconsistent parts of our personalities that do not bring glory to him.

Constant criticism

If you are like me you may find it hard to accept what sometimes feels like a constant barrage of criticism from your teenager. You may react: 'Who does he think he is, saying that about me?' For the time being resentment and anger blinds you to the possible truth in what has been said. It may be that your teenager is criticising you with more emotion than thought, but it is possible that he is right. On the other hand when he turns on you, resentful and hostile, it is possible that he is showing you more about himself than about yourself. His attack on you may be a mask, or a cover-up, for his feelings of inadequacy and doubt. While he criticises you aloud, he may be silently criticising himself in his heart. If you turn on him and retaliate, giving as good as you got, then you can harm him far more than you may realise. Your teenager cannot articulate his need for your affirmation and your support. The words cannot be expressed. He feels desperately doubtful about himself, and needs your full support rather than criticism at this time. This is a hard lesson for parents to remember when they feel they are under attack.

Your teenager longs to be accepted for himself, and he is usually willing to adapt where necessary to make this possible. If he makes a meal for the family in an effort to help, and you mutter a few casual words about 'super supper', and then spend the rest of the evening complaining that he has left the kitchen in a dreadful mess, can you be surprised if he feels discouraged? In the long run he must learn to clear up, but wait a while before taking him that further step. He may feel it is hopeless, he cannot do anything right, and that there is little point in trying. The more you criticise, the worse he will feel. Your teenager will grow increasingly discouraged, and the two of you will be trapped in a vicious circle unless you deliberately take yourself in hand and stop. It requires little initiative on your part to break the deadlock: just the words 'Well done, I like that!'

Christians have the biblical pattern of fatherly love to follow; the pattern of an ideal to strive for. We are to love and to accept our children in the way that God himself loves and accepts us; a standard that is so high that we are frightened even to try, but try we must. God loves the unlovely and he has no favourite children.

Saying 'Sorry'

None of us parents are perfect, and we find our tempers flare up in the face of criticism. Anger is sometimes a good thing. However, we may find we say things we should never have said, using words that are not only hurtful but are also untrue. A quick temper may prove a problem for the parent of teenagers. The only way I have found I can handle the aftermath of my unjust wrath is to eat a huge helping of humble pie, and go to my teenager and say: 'I'm sorry . . .' I regret that I have not done this as often as I should have. Yet, the times when I have asked forgiveness for unkind words have taught me that it is as important for me as it is for my children that I should learn to apologise to them.

25

Experiencing Jesus for himself

During this stage of development your child will be looking for meaning to life. He will already have scrutinised you, his parents. He may have found a certain elusive quality in your lives that he longs to possess himself, or he may have looked and found you wanting. As Christians you will long for him to see Jesus Christ shining in such clarity in your lives that he will follow, not you and your beliefs, but Jesus Christ himself as the Lord of his life, as well as of yours.

Try to be very patient with your teenager. Let him find Jesus for himself. Do not encourage his faith in God just as an extension of your own faith. His spiritual development may mean that he needs to distance himself from you and possibly from your faith, so that in the end, he will return to your faith as his very own — when he will experience Jesus in a unique way, and the reality of his faith can be independent of yours.

Trailing along to church

If your teenagers are among those who enthusiastically attend church, prayer meetings, and have to be removed from Bible study to do homework, then be grateful. And be careful not to criticise other families that are different from yours. You are not superior to them. There is no infallible way for Christian parents to bring up their children so that they are guaranteed to dedicate their lives to God. God's work of grace has to take place in individual hearts, and these works of grace frequently start in Christian homes and through the lives of Christian parents. If your teenager prefers not to attend church with the family you may wisely decide to make the minimum fuss about this and let him stay at home. But you will need to sort yourself out on this. It is easier for most of us to try to insist that our teenagers trail along with us to church than it is to give them the freedom of choice not to go if they request this.

I remember my acute embarrassment when I was a missionary on furlough in England some years ago and

26

my children opted not to go to church. Up to their early teens it was accepted in our family that they were expected to come with us but after that they knew that although we liked them to come we would not insist. In certain churches I was cross-examined about my children's 'spiritual state' (they were all pre-teen or early teens at that stage). I developed an almost paranoic feeling that these conversations would lead to me trying to justify why my children did or did not go to church. And the end result was that I felt an examined and failed parent. Make sure you do not fall into that trap.

Don't force your teenagers to go to church for no better reason than that you want to be respected and admired by others in the church. Getting your teenagers there by emotional blackmail will be resented later. Beware of this even more if you are a minister. It is tough for you, if as the leader of the flock you do not seem to be leading even your own children into the church. But, provided you are sure the Holy Spirit is guiding and giving you the assurance, stand firm. Remember that by pushing your teenagers through the doors of the church at a certain stage of their spiritual development you may be contributing to their rejection of the kingdom of heaven later. Their entry into the kingdom of heaven may be made easier if you do not shove them through a church door for a certain period of time.

You may feel 'good' and proud if your teenagers are there beside you — mute and resentful though they may be. People may admire you and your family. Yet the price paid in terms of a child's spiritual life can be too high, and you may eventually regret it.

Teen culture

Having a teenager around the house will make you only too aware that he is the target of the teenage mass market. Manufacturers have been quick to spot that today's teenager has money in his pocket. It angers me to see advertisements implying that certain cosmetics or certain clothes will turn a person lacking in self-assurance into a hunky hero or glamorous girl with friends swooning at their feet. I believe that the vulnerability of teenagers is exploited to line the pockets of some manufacturers, and I think it is morally wrong for adults to exploit teenage weakness for their own financial gain.

Along with the teenage mass market goes the teen mass culture. This is less easily defined. It is rarely communicated to children through their friends. More often, it is relayed through the media — magazines, tv and radio. This is not a complete culture in itself. Your teenager can belong to the teenage subculture through his radio and cassette player — a world different from yours — as well as being a fully integrated member of the culture in which your whole family lives. It is a world that often finds expression through teenage music, which gives little design for living and has virtually no religious, political or economic content. You will find that it functions only in your child's leisure time, and has little or no relevance to the real world of school, home or work.

Feelings

As an adult you will have learned to keep your feelings to yourself; the British stiff upper lip and all that! You may feel that there is something vaguely 'not nice' about displaying emotions in public. You have probably been trained and taught this way since childhood. You will feel deeply about certain things but tend not to share your feelings with other people. On the other hand, your teenager is living for his feelings. In his friendships he may be involved at an intense personal level and will often express his feelings about people rather than ideas or things.

You will tend to be moved by reason. Your teenager will tend to be moved by emotion. This is why he is more involved in poetry, art and music than most adults are. He may express his feelings impulsively, where you carefully plan beforehand. Up to a certain point, you can expect him to be idealistic, poetic and slightly wayward.

But you must draw a line at delinquency — society cannot cope with teenage delinquency.

Most teenagers are idealists. They are looking for something to capture them completely so that they can give their lives unreservedly to that cause or person. Don't dampen this enthusiasm. Life, later on, will teach them the unkind lesson that teenage ideals do not always match reality. For the time being, leave your teenager to dream his dreams and explore his ideals; they are an important part of developing a rounded personality.

Daydreaming is a normal part of your teenager's emotional development. Most girls go through a phase of identifying with the heroine in magazines, books and film stories; such romantic dreams are important. Boys tend to identify with heroic figures in the fields of athletics, adventure and romance. The thoughtful Bible-loving teenager may even identify with Bible characters, and may understand aspects of Jesus' life that you, a mere adult, have overlooked. Most teenagers realise underneath that their daydreams don't match up to reality, and they do not need you to tactlessly disillusion them. If you guess their daydreams then never let them realise this, never laugh at them, and never share these dreams with anyone else. They are secret and very private thoughts.

Letting go

One of the hardest things facing parents of teenagers is knowing when to let go and release control in certain areas of life, and when to hang on a little longer. You need to know your child well enough to be able to assess when he is able to handle which responsibilities alone: and as no two children are exactly alike no clear guidelines or definite ages can be given. This is just as hard for your teenager. He has to learn what to do in the tension he faces between dependence on you and being dominated by you, and between being free from you and living as an independent person in his own right.

Your aim is to help your child to develop as a mature

adult who can function without you, and the pathway between dependence and independence is a tough one for all concerned.

Of infinite value

Your teenager is at an important stage in life. He faces the prospect of having to grow up, to grow away from you, and finally to leave his family home. This is something that half of him longs to do and yet the other part of him cannot yet face. Your job is to stand by him as he learns to stand on his own. Your job is to have such confidence in him that his feelings of inferiority are lost in the assurance that you, his parents, think him of infinite value as a person. Above all, your job as Christian parents is to make it as easy as possible for your teenager to find God, who alone will give his life true meaning and purpose.

You, as a parent, face crises yourself as you come to terms with middle-age. But do not let your own problems stand in the way of your teenager, preventing him from developing his full potential as the unique adult God designed him to be.

3: The importance of independence

'Mum . . .' she said with one of her quizzical looks, 'It's me that's having problems with you — not you having problems with me!' Such words would probably be repeated thousands of times, in hundreds of homes, where parents think that they are having trouble in understanding their teenagers, without seeing that their teenagers also face major problems with their parents.

Parents with problems

It may come as a startling thought to you that you might be causing your teenager more problems than he is giving you. If you do not believe this, then take a long, hard look at the problem pages in women's magazines. Then take an even longer and harder look at the magazines aimed specifically at the teenage market. And if you make genuine efforts to see yourself as your teenage children see you, then you may discover that instead of epitomising perfect parenthood, you could be causing trouble for your growing children. You may come to the uncomfortable conclusion that it is not just other parents that are problems, it is virtually all of us. This is a sober thought that is worth bringing out into the open, because we can do a lot to make ourselves easier parents for our teenagers to cope with.

However, it's almost impossible to see yourself as your teenager sees you. For one thing, his opinions vary from day to day! Because he is passing through a stage when he finds it hard to understand what is happening inside himself, he may behave as an adult one minute, and the next do something so childish that you cannot believe it has been done by the same person. Although he probably does not realise it, your teenager is having to re-think some of the foundations on which his life is built. Matters that you assume settled spring to life again in his questioning mind. He is having to re-ask himself painful basic questions like: 'Can I trust my environment?', 'Who dare I reveal the real me to — is there anyone I can trust that far. . . ?'

You, a parent, will be looking at this from a different angle. As your teenager seeks someone with whom he feels secure enough to reveal his real self, you probably react: 'But surely it's obvious. We know you and love you. You can be your real self with us. There's no need for you to share with anyone else. . . .' But your teenager will see things differently. He now needs to grow up and develop apart from you. His unique personality is forming. This must be established in its own right, and not as an extension of yours. Therefore, no matter how much he loves and respects you, as his parent, you may still be the last person in whom he wants to confide.

You may react to this change in relationships in a very human way. You may feel: 'I know and love my child better than anyone else. He ought to share with me at such a crucial stage in his life . . . and if he doesn't open up to me then it means that I have failed as a parent . . .' But being the good parent of a teenager is not measured in terms of your closeness to each other. You do not 'pass or fail' in this subject. A good parent is often the one who is able to allow a growing teenager the freedom to develop away from him. He is one who cuts loose apron strings, and refuses attachment when there should be freedom and independence.

Even if you embody the ideal, wise and tactful parent, your own teenager still needs a break from you, for at least part of the time, as he develops. This break need not necessarily entail leaving home, but it does mean freedom not to have to share himself with you. He must be given the opportunity to grow in his own right.

The right friends
Your teenager does need the right friends. Pray hard that he will find the right confidants. Pray that God will give him friends of his own age or older with whom he can safely share himself, and through whom his full potential can develop. Pray for him to meet men and women who understand and accept young people and what is going on inside them.

When your child finds an adult in whom he can confide other than you then never attempt to extract confidences from that person. Curiosity and caring concern make you want to know what is going on inside your child, but make it a rule never to question any other adult who is helping him. Pray, and then trust the Holy Spirit, living within and guiding that other person, to speak as God wants your teenager spoken to. This is hard but necessary advice to well meaning, loving parents.

Whatever happens, don't start sulking if you discover that your teenager is closer to another adult then he is to you — some parents manage to do this! Be grateful that God has given your child someone to whom he can securely relate, and who he can trust. Mothers need to be careful not to be jealous if a teenage daughter forms a friendship with another woman the mother's own age. It is natural to long for your daughter's affection, but it is not very nice to resent it when her affection is deflected from you to others. Don't do this. Rejoice! Your daughter needs an older women with whom she can share. You probably want her friendship but it is not available to you for the moment. If you can wait patiently for a few years then your daughter will return to you and the two of you will have a richer friendship and closer relationship because you freed her from binding ties at the time she needed to grow apart.

Most mothers long for the time when a daughter will

grow up to become a friend also. This is very natural and very human, but avoid rushing things too fast. Otherwise you risk spoiling what would be richly yours if you let events take a slower course.

Keeping your distance

One day your teenager may confide in you with the openess he displayed when he was little. A week later he is tight-lipped, and so silent you fear you have inadvertently offended him. Of course, you may have offended him. You can hurt him in many ways. There is nothing that hurts a teenager more than the parent who tells everyone everything. 'If I tell you, then the whole church will know within a week!' one teenager muttered to his mother. True or not was beside the point, which was that this teenager (like all others) needed to rest assured that confidences would be respected, and that secrets would not be shared.

So try not to pressurise your teenager to share with you as he did when he was little. This may be very hard if, as a family, you have always shared everything. If your teenager stops sharing it does not imply he has no trust in you, nor that you have upset him. It merely indicates that he is growing up quite normally, and needs the opportunity to think separately from you. Do not invade the mental privacy your child needs or try to penetrate his thoughts unless he invites you to. Be available to him so that he can share, if he wants to, but never try to prise his secrets from him.

Handling yourself

We are all different as parents, and at this stage we may feel very insecure in our relationships with our teenagers. Some parents may not realise that they have depended on their children for their own emotional satisfaction. They have loved being the recipients of their children's confidences, and have needed to be needed. If you are such a parent you will find this stage of life bleak and hurtful. Your teenager apparently no longers needs you, and you may feel unwanted, useless and even rejected — you can be swamped in a sea of self-pity. Ignore what your child does or does not say to you. At this time words may be irrelevant. Rest secure in the fact that teenagers need their parents very much at this stage of life. They do not require more than occasional mothering, and no smothering, but it is essential for them to be assured of their parents' respect and value of them. Vital as you are to this transitional stage of your teenager's development, you may have to accept that you will not derive the same type of emotional satisfaction from exercising love for a teenager as you did for a toddler.

When you feel unwanted and unappreciated then stop looking at yourself and try and see what is going on inside your child. Try to forget yourself, and your personal desires and emptiness. Concentrate on your teenager and his needs. Then focus your whole being on trying actively to love him: that is, working towards his highest good. If you are doing this then you are loving him, in the biblical sense, with *agape* — love: the kind of loving that God asks of Christians. If you are able to look at this rationally and not emotionally, then sense may win the day. The best for your teenager is that he should develop as an adult who is independent of you. So, free him to do just that!

Remember that this process has nothing to do with you personally. You may assume that your child does not like you, or that he no longer loves you. This is not only the wrong time, but the worst time, to wonder about such things. Your child may not particularly like you at the moment (who does like a bossy mum, or work-swamped dad?) But within a few years your child could develop into one of your closest friends. Don't take any teenager's remarks too personally, or be hurt by what is said, or left unsaid. Thanks or words of appreciation, may be conspicuous by their absence.

Decision-making

'I've been through it all, and I don't know why he won't listen to me!' a red-faced father turned to me in exasperation. The trouble with some of us parents is that because we have lived longer than our teenagers, and because we have learned from our mistakes, we assume that we have a right, and possibly even an obligation, to pass on what we have learned to our children. In many senses this is absolutely true. We learn so that we can teach our children. God teaches us so that we can live what we learn, and also share it. But in many senses our children, and especially our teenagers, have to learn through personal experience, and that entails us granting them freedom to make mistakes.

I believe that I must share with my teenagers what experience has taught me, but having done that I must allow them to think through the implications of what I have learned, to draw their own conclusions. Obviously, at times, as a parent, you see disaster looming up in so dramatic a form that you must intervene to prevent it. But usually it is 'safe' to allow your teenager to make mistakes. He will learn from this experience. If you cocoon him, making all his decisions for him, have you prepared him adequately to face adult life? I think not. Your job is to stand at a distance and — often painfully — let your teenager learn how to make decisions apart from you. You will see him being hurt, and you will see him making silly mistakes, but you need to accept that this is a necessary part of growing up. He will then be capable of deciding for himself in major decisions. Remember that he is the person who has to live his own life. He is the one who must decide on career, marriage, and his own religious pathway. You cannot decide those for him. Teach him young about decision-making and he will then face his own major crossroads confident that he can safely make decisions for himself. And he will also know that he has to carry any repercussions himself from making wrong decisions.

If you make all the major decisions for your teenager

then you may find that this backfires on you. Your apparently acquiescing teenager may decide at a conscious, or unconscious level: 'OK! Dad's decided that I've got to take 'O' level Latin. I'm good at Latin and I could do well at it. But I'm going to show him who's running my life by failing Latin magnificently!' I know one girl who did just that in 'O' level Chemistry. Some teenagers who turn out to be the opposite of all that their dominant parents decided they should be, can be acting out unexpressed feelings: 'If I'm going to be bad in their eyes then I'm going to excel in being bad! If I'm a failure to them I'll excel at failing!' This is a sad and silly situation, and dominant parents can avoid it by being wise before, and not after, the event.

His territory

Another area where you are wise to keep out of your teenager's life is in his bedroom, and with his possessions. When he was little he probably couldn't care less if you cleared and cleaned his room. By the time your child is a young teenager he will probably have developed an attachment to certain things; to possessions that are his very own. The things that he loves are likely to be the things he has chosen and bought for himself. They rarely include what you have selected for him and given him as presents.

For this reason, be careful not to clear out your teenager's collections of (what appears to you to be) rubbish. These odd bits and pieces from his life are important and valuable to him. He expresses his emerging personality through his collection of precious objects. Do not carry out your slum-clearance act on his bedroom. You will throw out his treasures if you do so, he will resent it greatly, and your relationship will be impaired. Not only will you have intruded into his private collection of treasures but you will have failed to respect his developing personhood and maturing adulthood. He will also not appreciate younger brothers and sisters going through his possessions. Try and keep siblings away from the possessions of the older ones.

'Her bedroom is a disgrace!' several parents have complained to me. 'How can anyone live in such a pigsty? The only time her room gets cleaned, is when one of us goes in and does it!' Most parents tend to shudder at the sight of their teenager's room. Some feel that this mess is an affront to the respectable house they are running. Some might even agree that their middle-class ideals of respectability have been challenged by this one room existing in the state in which it does! If your teenager's room is like this then you may wonder how he will ever manage to run a house of his own later on, if he cannot keep even one room tidy. It is amazing how virtually all teenagers grow up, marry, and then succeed in running clean, tidy houses, despite the way they failed to care for their bedrooms as teenagers!

You can cause major rows and friction in your house if you lay down the law and insist that your teenager keeps his room as you decide it should be kept. Whose room is it? His or yours? Whose house is he living in? Yours — yes — but it is also his home. If it really is his home too then is there any valid reason why he should not have the little part of the house — his room — as he wants it? Provided it isn't over-run with rats carrying plague (which it won't be) is it really necessary even to ask him to keep his things tidy? If he drops his clothes on the floor, and they lie there getting creased, then they will be in that state when he next needs them — provided you don't unhelpfully go and pick up, and wash and iron behind him. He will soon learn what happens to clothes left in a mess and it will save you hours of nagging and valuable stores of energy.

The act of keeping his room as you don't like it is one rather harmless way of asserting independence, of saying: 'I'm me and I want to be me in my room!' This is not usually a serious act of rebellion requiring a heavy-handed father, such action merely kindles unnecessary, and probably non-existent, hostility.

If your teenager has his own room and needs to feel independent, then he might appreciate it if his bedroom was turned into a bed-sitting room, where he could be during the day and night. He might appreciate having a lock on the door: not so that he can do anything you might forbid behind locked doors, but simply to feel that he was free to be himself without you trampling in on his privacy unannounced, at any time you wanted to. While your teenager is discovering himself he needs time and space to be on his own, where he can retreat from the family. Imagination can transform even shared bedrooms into little havens of privacy where brothers and sisters are not allowed to intrude. Use all your gifts of creativity to give him such a haven when he needs it, even the simplest of partitions can help.

No wonder many teenagers feel that they have trouble in coping with their parents. While they are struggling to be independent it's easy for parents to thoughtlessly refuse to free them to be themselves. And it is in such mundane matters as untidy bedrooms that vital issues like growing into adult independence are worked out.

Knowing the law

I trust that you will never need to know the law in relation to your teenagers. As a mother though I find that it is useful information to know because you cannot allow your child to break the law without saying something to try and stop him. If your teenager is questioned by the police then he does not have to answer them but he is wise to do so politely and truthfully. He breaks the law if he gives a false name and address. If he is arrested then he will be allowed out on bail unless a police chief thinks it is safer for him to be detained, or if he is suspected of a serious crime, or if the police think he will jump bail. He must be taken to court within 72 hours.

If your teenager is sixteen and working then you cannot usually make him live at home. Yet according to British law you can make him go to school until he is eighteen! A couple cannot marry until they are aged sixteen. Under eighteens usually need parental permission to do so, but a court order can be given instead. Your child may leave school at sixteen. Under this age he is not allowed to smoke in public, nor to buy cigarettes. If caught by the police then the police can take away the cigarettes. There is no law to stop your child smoking at any age — he mustn't be caught, that's all!

A boy can legally have intercourse with a woman at any age. The legal age of consent for a girl is sixteen. A man having intercourse with a girl under sixteen is breaking the law. Homosexual intercourse is forbidden by law for a man under the age of twenty one. There is no similar law covering lesbian relationships for women. A girl having a sexual relationship under-age with a man could be taken to court and put into care, or a supervision order could be made.

Making a change

You may now understand why the agony columns in teenage magazines give so much space to the problems of coping with parents. Needless to say, your teenagers will find it hard to handle you if you cannot handle yourself. And it will be harder if you are unable or unwilling to release them to be the people that they were designed by God to be. Most teenagers want to please their parents. Although their parents may be a problem to them they still try to adapt and to fit in to please. Once parents are aware of the fact that they themselves may be more of a problem to their teenagers than their teenagers could ever be to them then life could change in the homes of many teenagers. And the agony aunties of the teen magazines might even find their work load reduced by half!

4: Conformity
and non-conformity

'My daughter is making life very uncomfortable for all of us . . .' his brow wrinkled, 'I wasn't ever like that when I was a teenager. . . ' Like many parents he found it hard to understand what life is like as a teenager today.

You may fail to see why one of the teenagers in your family insists on colouring his hair in pink and green stripes at weekends, only to wash the colours out in time for school early on Monday morning. You may not understand why your daughter delights in ferreting around in granny's attic and fishing out old-fashioned clothes from ancient trunks, to wear with obvious pleasure when she is with certain friends. But your lack of comprehension must never diminish your appreciation of your teenager's worth, nor should lack of comprehension be allowed to turn into unwarranted fear. Outer appearance does not always match inner worth.

Teenage gear
The teenager who dresses like his friends in what seems to you outlandish gear may be an ordinary, kind person under all his clothes. If your teenagers have friends who dress in punk outfits, then don't automatically assume that allowing them into your house means that it will be over-run with hooligans who will wreck everything. A group of teenagers in their gear does not necessarily spell trouble although media reports of families hurt by groups of youths might lead you to assume this is so. Be sensible about such groups, but don't be unduly fearful.

One of the gentlest and kindest teenagers I know taught me an invaluable lesson: not to judge by outer appearance alone. When I first visited his parents at home, words failed me — what does someone like me say to 'a punk'? I had no ideas and so said nothing to him and concentrated on chatting to the rest of the family, who were dressed in 'normal' clothes and usual hair styles. As the evening wore on, I noticed that the parents treated their 'punk' son with affection. In fact he did everything in exactly the same way as the rest of the family. To my surprise I found that by the end of that evening I had stopped seeing a boy in punk gear, and simply saw a boy. I discovered a sensitive and thoughtful person, and I realised how wrong I had been to pre-judge that teenager on clothes and hair alone.

Not your taste

A boy in a leather jacket with side-burns may be proclaiming: 'I'm an adult now, and I can choose for myself!' through his choice of dress and hair style. The girl who wears her hair in a freakish style, that her mother emphatically dislikes, is similarly declaring her independence.

If your teenager wears the strange uniform (in adult eyes) of some teenagers, then don't assume that he will be a drop-out from society. He has not analysed why he is wearing these clothes. But he will derive comfort from them. Merely wearing such outfits will reassure him that he is growing up, and that he is just like the others who are growing up around him. For some teenagers these clothes spell the reassurance that they are not an oddity, or malformed, or the freak that they sometimes fear they are.

I see little point in fighting a battle with your child over his teenage gear. Even if you win this battle, you will lose an important war. If you understand why he wants, or even needs, to dress in this way, then you may find his clothes more acceptable. The neighbours or your fellow church members may not understand why your teenager dresses as he does but surely your child is more important than anything anyone thinks. You can cause unnecessary emotional battles over clothes, and lead your teenager away from you instead of keeping him with you through his teenage years if you act unwisely.

Try to analyse your reactions to your teenager's unusual clothes and hair style. Why don't you like it? Possibly because you think it doesn't suit him. Possibly you are embarrassed that he doesn't conform to others around you. Think hard, and try to see if at the root of your feelings lies frustration that you are powerless to force your child to dress as you want him to: this is one way in which your teenager can defy you. It is one way in which he ought to be freed to express his independence. If you are wise you will free him from any need to defy you. Let him dress as he chooses out of school and work. It is harmless, and may even do him good! It is some consolation that teenage gear is expensive, so he will not be able to afford much, and also, most people grow out of teenage clothes when they become adults! After a few years a teenager no longer needs to express his independence in this way.

Gangs and groups
A major fact that the adult world finds hard to face is teenage gangs. This is hardly surprising. Almost every week the media seem to describe a group of teenagers who have mugged an old lady outside the post office, wrecked other people's property, or run wild with motor bikes on beaches on a Bank Holiday. Your teenager may, or may not, be involved with a gang. Whether he is or not, it is important for you to understand why groups play an important part in the life of most teenagers.

Watch your teenager carefully, and ask yourself the question: 'Who has the most influence on my teenager — his family or his friends?' You may be surprised to have to admit that those who most influence him are others of his own age, and usually those of the same sex. They have chosen one another because they share the same basic values and are able to relate to one another as equals. They will tend to spend their free time together with boys usually going round in groups of around five or so. In a gang each member may behave quite differently than if he was on his own. You are bound to have heard parents state in bewilderment: 'But my boy just isn't like that . . . he'd never do the things those boys did . . . I can't think what got into him'. Their puzzled comments express an important truth, because the psychology of gang behaviour is different from that of the behaviour of individuals. Sometimes members of a gang will try to impress the others by rejecting the rules of behaviour they know, as individuals, to be acceptable. The one who rejects authority may feel bolstered by the knowledge that he is acting on behalf of the other members of his group, and not just for himself alone.

Never mentally write off gangs and groups as totally bad. Your son may need to belong to such a group. The more he lacks self-confidence and a feeling of self-worth, the more he is going to try to be like his group. It is only the secure teenager, who is certain of his self-worth, who can stand out against his friends and say: 'You may do that but I'm not going to. I think it's wrong. . .'

The drive to belong is so strong in a teenager that for some it becomes a way of life. He may need, if he is shy and retiring, to be in the company of others who are more daring. The others in the group give reassurance that the problems being faced by one member are not unique, and that they all face the same things to different degrees. Your teenager will learn from the others how to overcome the problems he encounters. In these groups it is important that all are equal. It is an unwritten law, and understood by all, that no one person takes too much lead, and no one person gets too big for his boots. This means that a father cannot be 'one of the boys'. He might contribute to the life of his sons and their friends very positively but he can never really be one with them.

It is important to teenagers that they are loyal to the group to which they belong. Loyalty to this group of friends is usually put before loyalty to family, school, youth group and other claims on loyalties. If your teenager puts friends before family then try not to feel betrayed. He is behaving normally and it is right for teenagers to support one another in this way. They need the solidarity that comes from belonging to one another. They need to be accepted by others of their own age group, and they give and expect loyal support.

You will find by contrast that your daughters naturally and rightly tend to gain moral support from one or two very close girl friends. Their relationships may seem very intense to you. Teenagers live on an emotional plane and normally tend to form friendships that are more intense than adult ones. Be careful not to jump to the wrong conclusion that your daughter has a lesbian tendency when she is merely experiencing the richness of a healthy teenage friendship.

In the close group of two or three friends, girls will share close confidences and boost one another's flagging morale. Together they will encourage one another to experiment with new things like make-up, boyfriends, clothes, new hair styles, and sometimes a small revolution against authority. Watch your daughter and her friends if they decide to rebel or question the authority of one member of staff at school. Two or three girls can make life impossible for one teacher if they club together against him or her in this way, and your daughter may need your help in understanding how much she is hurting that teacher, and even harming her career.

Probably you shudder at your daughter's choice of friend. Even if you are silent you may think: 'What can she see in that girl. They're so different . . .' In fact, you have answered your own question. It is likely that your daughter has chosen as her 'best' friend someone who is totally different from her. Each sees in the other qualities that they themselves are lacking, and choose as close friends — at this stage — those who compensate for their own weaknesses. This may mean that long-standing friends are dropped for a few years; but it is probable that the old friends will return at the end of teenage years and be the friends that remain close throughout life.

This is one of many good reasons why you cannot choose friends for your teenagers, who will be seeking qualities that you would never think of. That 'nice girl next door' or the 'pleasant boy from church' probably won't be right for your teenager as he finds his own feet. You will fail, and cause embarrassment, if you try to force friendships — it rarely works at this age.

Conflicting views

Your teenager's views and friends are areas of potential conflict. He and his friends may hold ideals, and do things, that you feel are unacceptable for members of your family. These may involve major matters, or may be relatively small but important things like the time in which you expect him home at night.

It will not help your teenager if you compromise your integrity on important matters of principle, and pretend that you don't mind certain things going on when really you do. Your teenager does need the reassurance of knowing that you still hold to the standards in which you have brought him up, and he needs the security of knowing this does not change. On the other hand, it is not always necessary to stick to petty ideas of your own, and to disagree violently every time your teenager sees differently. You do not have to prove to him that you are still the boss! If he wants to put chocolate sauce on his fried eggs instead of tomato ketchup does it really matter? You will probably find that you are able to forget or ignore some of the ways you think and behave in order to adapt to your teenager's lifestyle, and equally you can expect him to give way to you as well. If you are able to do this then you will lessen possible friction between you and your child. Give and take on both sides makes for harmony. This has the added bonus that your teenager may then bring his friends home if he knows that it is likely that you and he will get on all right while they are there. If he knows that a clash between the two of you is possible or even inevitable when his friends are at home then he will not invite them home. It is in your interests to get to know your child's friends, if you possibly can.

Try not to allow a conflict of loyalties to flare up into a burning issue in your teenager's life. Try not to precipitate situations in which he has to choose between you or his friends. This is usually unnecessary. For his development he needs both his friends and his family so try to ensure he has both. Most teenagers find their own way out of conflicting situations and will then try to keep friends and family in separate compartments of their lives.

Divided loyalties

I shall never forget the afternoon that Jean came to see me. I have always thought of her as being the mother of perfect children; the kind of model mother who would never face any difficulties with her family — and certainly the kind of person I could never never match. Her eyes were dark-rimmed as she spilled out her story: 'It's about Mary . . .' her words faltered as she told me about her nineteen year old daughter, 'I never really liked her friends but I couldn't stop her going out with that Freda. I didn't know what they did all the time they were out. I knew that Mary had started smoking but I didn't know she was on drugs . . . we kept on having rows about Freda because I never trusted her.' She paused, and looked hard at the floor, 'Now Mary's going . . . she's leaving home just like that, and says she's going to get a job and share a flat with Freda . . . ' My heart went out to Jean.

How could such a thing happen to such a perfect mother? It could happen to her because it could happen to any parent. If you make your child choose between you and their friends then you may force your child to assert his developing adulthood in a way that he might otherwise not have chosen to do. And, at a stage when he would prefer not to, he may opt for loyalty to friends instead of family.

It is usually possible by tactful handling not to allow this kind of situation to occur between you and your teenager. Even if you dislike his friends and what they do, refrain from excessive comment. Try not to allow yourself, or your teenager, to be forced in the position where either side makes an ultimatum that he will have to leave home if this or that doesn't stop. No matter how far your teenager seems to be separated from you in his outlook on life, remember that he still needs you. The time will almost certainly come when he needs somewhere safe to which he can retreat, when the world has become bigger and more frightening than he can handle on his own. That place ideally should be his own home with his own parents. Make sure that you and your home are always there for your teenagers, no matter how far they seem to have gone from you. If you are unconvinced or undecided about taking a 'wayward' son or daughter back home again then I believe your debate should be short-lived. Pick up your Bible and read Jesus' story of the prodigal son. God will show you clearly through this story what attitude you, a Christian, should have.

Coping with conflict

It is likely that your teenager is more anxious to avoid conflict with you, than you are with him. You may have the parental attitude of: 'Let's get some sense hammered into his thick skull . . . ', or, even expressed less vehemently than this you may still adopt the same attitude. Be careful of it, as you may drive your teenager away from you; neither he nor you really wants that to happen. Your teenager knows your standards and he will know only too well if he is doing things that would upset you, if you found out. He will do his best to hide things that he is doing that you would disapprove of (and you might be wise to ignore secrets you discover) unless they are put there deliberately for you to discover.

I remember another friend, Joyce, telling me that she

routinely turned out her son's jacket pockets before she sent his suit to the cleaners. James, her son, knew she did this and had removed nearly everything from the pockets. As Joyce checked she absent-mindedly pulled out something left in one pocket. She disinterestedly looked down to see what was there, and froze. In James' pocket she had found a contraceptive sheath. Her immediate reaction was emotional. How could her seventeen year old even know what condoms were, let alone own them? By the time James was home from school, she had worked out her strategy. She tapped gently on his bedroom door while he was doing his homework. He looked up hesitantly: 'Hi mum!' She held out her hand, opened it, and said: 'I found this in your pocket. I hope you won't need it and so I'm throwing it away'. After a slight pause she added, 'Supper in half an hour . . . ' and was gone.

I happened to talk to James about this several years later. 'It was a turning point for me', he shared. 'My friends had encouraged me to buy a packet of them, so I did. But I didn't want to have to be like them. I didn't really want to have to sleep with a girl till we married. I half hoped that mum would find that condom and that she'd give me the courage to say "no" to my friends. The fact that she said so little, but showed so clearly what she thought, meant more than she'll ever know. I never slept with a girl till I married. . .'

Joyce had discovered a secret that parents of teenagers need to find for themselves. The secret of how to keep lines of communication open when there are areas of major conflict and disagreement.

What does God want?
If your teenager seems to be developing into all that you hoped he would not be, then do not give up hope. Pray, pray and still pray for him. You can rest assured that God loves him more than even you do. And God longs that your child will find the abundance of life that is available in Jesus to those who live in him. As you focus

your prayers on your teenager try not to pray that your teenager will conform to a certain type of person. Life is not really about this. You are not asking God to turn your teenager into a typical suburban middle-class business man, who lives in a respectable box-like house in a row of other little boxes, catches the 7.45 every day for the city, and returns on the 6.15 in time for a deacons' meeting in the evening at church! You should not pray for your child to conform to any type. You should be asking God for your child to start off on a spiritual pilgrimage that will culminate with the most glorious climax possible — that of discovering the reality of the living God, and of dedicating the potential and power of his life to him. You are not praying for your teenager to become a certain type of person, rather you are praying for him to encounter Jesus — the one person who will take his life and fill it with the rich meaning and depth of colour that life in Christ takes on for the Christian.

Remember too that you are not praying just for the fruit of the Spirit (love, joy, peace, long suffering, gentleness, goodness, faithfulness and self-control) to appear in your child's life, without your child first experiencing the Holy Spirit for himself! You can pray, 'Dear God, please help him to be patient with dad today or there'll be ructions. . .', but you cannot assume that supernatural gifts will appear (gifts that God alone can give) without God himself doing something special in your child's heart. For your child's life to realise its full potential he, like all of us, must know God and grow into an ever deepening personal relationship with him. Focus your praying on this, rather than on the by-products that develop as a bonus of such a transforming relationship. Don't ask God to give your child carts before he has given him horses!

Beneath the surface
Learn to look beneath the surface and to understand your teenager. As you do this you will see much of worth that you may otherwise fail to appreciate. You must tell

him how valuable he is, because he needs your support and reassurance of his worth at this stage of life.

Look, see, and share with him — and you and he will grow in mutual understanding and respect.

5: The value of disagreement

I was at a loss to know what to say so I remained silent,
listening to her monologue with an impassive face: 'Of
course our Judy has always been a perfect daughter.
We've never had any worry with her. . .' and so it went
on.

What could I say? I could hardly reply: 'Are you
blind? If you've not been worried sick about your Judy,
then I have! Don't you know what's going on?' She was
obviously unaware of what was happening in her daughter's life, and I could not enlighten her. Judy had shared
the problems of being a teenager with me. Her mother
knew about this and together we agreed that none of
Judy's secrets would pass from me to her parents. Her
mother had wanted it that way. So she knew nothing of
the double-life Judy led. At home she played the role of
perfect daughter; always obedient, placid and helpful.
Away from home she led a life that was the opposite of
all her parents imagined and wanted her to be.

Over-reaction
What do you do if you unexpectedly discover that your
teenager is doing things that you feel he should not do?
If you over-react, you may drive these activities under-
ground; and yet paradoxically if you remain silent he
may wish you had expressed some disapproval so that
he knew that you still felt as he imagined you would.
You know your teenager, and your intuitive sense of
what is right for him may be the best guide if a situation
like this should arise.

Remember though that your child is still loyal and

loving to you, even if he appears to be the opposite! The reason that he hides some of the things he does, so that you won't discover them, may be out of loyalty to you. He may not want you to find out and be hurt; and yet he may still need to try out things he knows you dislike, in order to work out for himself what he will, and what he will not, do as an adult.

If you make enough fuss about something that he does as an experiment, you may even manage to turn that thing into a permanent way of life for him. Be on guard against doing this! If you catch your son smoking at the bottom of the garden, and you strongly disapprove of smoking, then you could make a major issue out of it. But instead of your teenager giving up smoking, you may force him to assert his independence, and to start smoking regularly, not at the bottom of the garden but in any room in the house that is not forbidden. Over-reaction when something is being done experimentally can have the opposite effect of what you wanted. You may find it very hard to sit back and do virtually nothing when your teenager is acting in a way that you are sure is not only wrong but is also harmful. Having gently shared your view don't remain totally inactive. You must take action, and as a Christian parent at this point you must act on your knees. Praying is hard work, and this is the time for you to exert yourself and to work with God in prayer for your child. Pray that your child will discover God in such a relevant way that the particular problem will be transformed into a side-issue to be later put right as your child lines his life up with God's plan for him.

Other families

At this stage in life, many teenagers try to decide whether or not they will adopt their parents' life style. This poses virtually no problems for you if your teenager just looks and thinks, but problems arise if he does the opposite to what you do — and takes action — to see what it feels like. You may be hurt at his involvement with families other than your own. 'You'd never think she had a good home to come home to', one mother summed it up. 'She spends all her time round at her friend's . . .' What that mother failed to realise was that her daughter needed to see what life was like in other families. She had grown up in a strict Christian family, within a framework of rigid ways and fairly tight rules. The girl needed to experience the type of life that went on in her friend's non-Christian home, so that she could know for herself what it was to live outside a Christian framework. If your Christian home is Christ-centred in practise as well as in words then you should not be afraid to let your children experience life in non-Christian homes. But you may be fearful for very good reasons. You may fear that your children will be drawn into situation that they are, as yet, unable to handle; and fear that they may drift into situations that they are, as yet, unable to handle; and fear that they may drift into something that will lead them astray. And more deeply, at the root of the unspoken fear of some Christian parents, is a valid fear that the quality of their Christian home-life leaves much to be desired.

There are other, simpler, reasons why your teenager may be spending a lot of time in another family. No one family can possibly supply everything that any one person needs. Your child may find in another family, things that are lacking in his own. He may learn to bird-watch, to sail, to repair television sets, and get help with 'A' level physics homework in a family other than his own; for the simple reason that you, like me, know nothing about these subjects. So, don't take this personally! Don't feel a rejected parent.

If your teenager has been with other families he may appear not only critical but also hostile to the environment you create in your home. Don't assume that he has to be wrong and you have to be right, if the two of you assess the quality of your family life differently. You may be a Christian family but you may not be creating the sort of Christian family life that God intends for your family. The situation may need your teenager to show you this. Try and be open-minded and ready to hear God speaking to you through your own teenager.

Sharing your failure

You could try asking yourself, 'Is my life so filled by the presence of the Holy Spirit that my children sense his presence, and his relevance in every situation?' Try answering that question in the silence of your own heart. If you are like me, you will see your failure. You will see that as a parent you have failed your child, by failing to live close to God. Yet God never leaves you and your children alone in failure, and if you come to God with your failure, seeking his forgiveness, then he does forgive. Even more, God heals and restores in broken relationships and situations of hurt. He restores not only at a personal level of you and him, but at a deeper level of God, you and your family.

If you pass through a period of letting God sort you out spiritually, then it may help all of you if you can be open enough to share it with your teenager afterwards. It will teach him much he needs to know about you, but more than that it will help him to understand God better. If your child knows that you see yourself as a failed parent, then he will judge you, and your quality of Christian home life, less harshly than if you pretend to be perfect when everyone knows that you are not. A situation like this could be the situation that makes your child decide in favour of adopting your Christian life style as his own. Probably the determining factor is your willingness to be honest not only with yourself (about what has happened in your spiritual life) but also your willingness to share this frankly with your teenager.

Family life with God

You will find that God has a lot to teach you about your family through the words of your family. Take a family's corporate spiritual life, for instance. I believe that many Christian families are impoverished because they have no corporate spiritual life, and teenagers may be the first people to point this out. Your generation has probably grown up to believe in a personal God and in the importance of developing a personal relationship with Jesus Christ. You seek to develop your private relationship with God in a very personal way by prayer, Bible reading and daily meditation. You may develop your spiritual lives as a married couple and grow together by sharing prayer and Bible reading together. But Christian families rarely involve their children deeply in a corporate spiritual family life, and your teenager may be the first person to show you this. It may come out in questions like: 'Dad when you bought this house, and said that God guided us to it, why didn't we all pray about it together . . . and why did God make me go to school I didn't want to go to just because you were guided to a certain house?' Your child could have known God's leading, to a new school and new friends, as clearly as you had to a new town and new house had you involved the family in corporate decision-making with God.

If you are in full-time Christian service your teenager may rightly question: 'Why haven't we as much money as my friends? Why aren't you doing a "proper" job like my friend's parents? Why am I involved in the cost of your job . . . it's costing me more than you because you enjoy it . . . ' Such a situation need not arise if a family decides before God to accept a certain calling as a family. But that sort of family spirituality does not arise from nowhere — it does not drop from heaven in crisis situations. It comes from a quality of family spirituality in which the family group learns to love, worship and grow in God as a group, as well as individuals. Your teenager may challenge your Christian family life, and prompt you to necessary action.

It will be harder for you if you are faithfully doing what you believe that God is asking of you as a Christian parent, if you have insisted on daily family prayers and Bible reading at breakfast, on certain prohibitions about the use of Sundays, and on a certain strict lifestyle that your teenager begins to question. At the bottom of his questioning may lie deep unspoken words like: 'Why is your Christianity so joyless, so rigid, and so uncreative and unloving?' He may not say those exact words because he may not want to hurt you. Read between the lines and listen to his silence. You may find that through your teenager God is showing you patterns of behaviour in your family that follow a certain Christian tradition for family life, but which are not God's pattern for all families.

You are going to have to decide, as parents, what is and what is not important for your family. You will be wise if you explain to your children why you insist on certain things, and you will then probably be able to carry them along with you.

Rules and regulations

For instance, there is no 'correct' or 'Christian' time for teenagers to be in at night. To listen to the rows in some homes you would feel that this was one of the issues of ultimate importance! Set a time for your teenagers to be in after a sensible and unemotive discussion with them about it. They need to know that you care whether they are in or not. If you wait up till they are in and then face the words: 'Don't you trust me to be in on time?' be careful how you react, no matter how tired you are. And don't turn the issue into tension between your authority versus your child's desire for independence. If your teenager is late home and you land up with a row about it in the middle of the night then discuss it again more calmly in the morning — when none of you are over-tired! Your teenagers need to realise that you are human enough to be frightened about them when they fail to appear at the agreed time. They need to know you love them enough to be concerned. It may be that you need to agree to be a little more flexible about the exact time for them to be home, so that anyone staying out later than the agreed time will telephone in advance giving warning. This should not be a matter of authority versus independence.

In today's world it is a matter of common sense. Your teenager knows as well as you do that non-appearance at home at night is a matter to be reported to the police for his (and others') safety.

Non-stop music

Another potential area of disagreement is that of music — teenage and adult music tastes do not often coincide. One reason is that music may fulfill a different role in your teenager's life than it does in yours. You may like to sit quietly listening to the intricacies of one conductor's handling of a piece of music, or enjoying the general tenor of the music as such. Your teenager may also do this, but it is more likely that music for him is a means of expressing his emotions. Remember that he is reacting on an emotional plane while you react on an intellectual plane. Music is one of the areas where this difference is apparent.

Pop music may give him an outlet to express his surging emotions, and these are better expressed than left submerged. His daily routine may seem dull, boring, colourless and flat. Pop music may add the dimension and expression of warmth and colour that his emotions demand. Part of his growing into an adult is learning how to handle his emotions, and music has a role to play in this.

His passion for non-stop music may drive you mad. The beat throbs relentlessly through the whole house, and you cannot escape it even if you flee to the bottom of the garden. For some strange reason it does not satisfy him unless it is loud — too loud for you! One way out is for you to buy him head-phones, because even wax ear-plugs won't keep that beat out of your brain!

You will probably find that your teenager has music on non-stop whether or not he is listening to it. He will think you rather odd if you suggest that he was listening to it! He can be studying or doing something absorbing while the music is on, and yet at the same time his subconscious mind can be deriving satisfaction from it.

Some teenagers will admit that the music helps them to escape from their own thoughts. This helps them if they are anxious about themselves, feel inadequate, or have a real or imagined worry. Music, in this case, is treating symptoms rather than the cause of a sort of illness — so don't encourage it for this reason alone.

You may be unable to understand the words of pop music, and you may therefore assume that your child cannot understand them either. Don't be deluded, he can understand. You may be wise to check the words on the record cover to see just what your teenager is listening to. A few groups have undertones of occult involvement that you will not want your teenager listening to, and once you have pointed this out to him he may agree and keep away from that record.

Since your teenager is able to understand the words of pop records you will find that he is also able to understand the words of those Christian pop singers who make a noise you find incomprehensible. Don't condemn this music out of hand. Some teenagers have found God through Christian pop music where God did not meet them in church, at home or anywhere else. Just because you do not find God in this type of music do not assume your teenager will not.

Sexual standards

Your major area of conflict with your teenager may well be in the area of sexual standards. You may be horrified to hear your child state categorically: 'It doesn't matter who you sleep with as long as you both want to and no one gets hurt'. He is repeating what he has heard around him, usually from his friends. He will find it reassuring when you state calmly, 'Mum and I believe in one man, one woman, for life — and we believe that this is God's ideal for everyone'.

At this stage try not to allow the authority issue to cloud your teenager's thinking. Don't make him jump into bed with someone to have to prove that he is independent of you. A tactless, excessively authoritarian parent could precipitate just such a reaction. Be careful not to speak in such a way that you criticise his friends' sexual standards. Never drive him into a corner where he is forced to declare loyalty to his friends, and to do this he has to prove his friends are right and you are wrong; and to do so he experiments sexually. Watch your words so that you do not precipitate this.

If your teenager is secure, and he knows that he has your quiet affirmation of him as a person of worth then he not only can, but probably will, stand out on certain issues and refuse to conform. This is difficult for him because it cuts right across his need to be accepted and to be like his peers.

Face reality together
It is hardly surprising that teenagers and adults face conflict. It is surprising that they don't face more! Your teenager feels that emotions are the most important factors in his life. He wants to be spontaneous, honest, free and dramatic. Those are good qualities to him. Your adult world is dominated by British reserve; there is uniformity, calculation, control, concealment and routine.

You need a sense of humour; to laugh at yourself and at the situation, but not at your teenager (he might be hurt). When he makes his dramatic, spontaneous bid for independence and does precisely the one thing that he knows will have maximum dramatic impact — lighting up a cigarette and announcing loudly in front of granny that he is going to the pub — then keep your reactions down until he has gone. And then laugh it out of your system.

The other factor that will bind you to your teenager is your willingness to reveal your humanness to him. He will respect you if you are open, honest and human to him. Don't over-do this though and don't embarrass him by using him as a kind of substitute father-confessor!

Your teenager will respect you if you admit that you have done wrong, or that you don't know something.

60

The trouble is that, being human, parents often over-react, and then have to live with the repercussions of what has been done or said. But you will find that your teenagers are far more forgiving than you credit them for. If you ask for forgiveness for saying harsh and unkind words in haste then you will find a depth of understanding that you possibly had not expected. And never fear that you will lose your teenager's respect if you apologise to him. You will gain far more respect for admitting that you were wrong. What he cannot forgive is the parent who refuses to admit that charges against him could possibly be true. Face reality with your teenager, don't retreat into authoritarianism, and then you will develop a deep and growing bond that will persist throughout life.

6: Parents in mid-life crisis

He looked me straight in the eye and said: 'The greatest gift any parents can give their children is that of having a happy and stable marriage themselves.' I should not have been surprised at his words but I was. When I thought carefully about it I found I agreed whole-heartedly. It sounded so obvious that I wondered how I could have overlooked it before, or have pushed it to the back of my mind.

Those words apply to all marriages, no matter what ages the children are. But if you take them and try to work them out in daily living you are likely to find you have a lot of sorting and working out to do as a married couple, especially at the stage of life you have reached when your children enter their teens.

Take yourself in hand

At the same time as children become teenagers many parents pass through a stage of adult life called the 'mid-life crisis'. For many people, the months or years of living through a mid-life crisis are painful and difficult. When this happens, you will need to take yourself in hand if you are going to build relationships at home with all the family and provide the security your children need.

Many women pass through an uncomfortable stage of reassessing themselves at about the age of thirty five (this has nothing to do with the menopause, which comes later), and men do the same around their fortieth birthday. But no two people are the same. If you have never hit this phase at the age given then don't worry; if it never happens to you then be grateful!

Men and dads

For most men, the forties are years of re-thinking and reassessing almost everything. Because life is tough for these years a man may be hard to live with. The rest of the family may even feel that they are living with two adolescents — the teenager and dad (or mum at a different time). Sometimes dad may burst into unpredictable fits of anger over a minor matter that would not have bothered him previously. At other times, he may withdraw into himself and seem depressed. He no longer presents the stability and security to the rest of the family that he used to. A father who has been the leader of the family may abdicate this leadership role and uncharacteristically leave major family decision-making to his wife. Instead of being the person on whom the family leans for support, he may turn to his wife for support and strength. This she may unwittingly refuse because she does not understand his needs. No wonder the family is confused. The question, 'What's up with dad?' remains unanswered because no one (least of all dad) understands what is happening. Few men anticipate a time like this, when they have either achieved what they set out to do, or realise they are not going to attain their goals. They do not expect to have to seek meaning to life all over again, to understand their identity and reassess their roles. In an adult way a husband can be re-evaluating his life now is half over, in a similar manner to his teenager.

A husband needs love and understanding if, and when, he passes through a mid-life crisis. Your husband is not being childish if he appears to change for no apparent reason, and no longer behaves at home as the man you have known him to be for years. Be quietly supportive. If he needs you to carry the load of decision-making at home for a time, then do this quietly, and be ready to hand it back to him when he is able to manage it again.

You know your man, and you know how best to help him through this stage, with minimum trauma to himself and to the rest of the family.

Make sure that your husband knows that you find him attractive sexually. Don't let him feel a failure in this part of his life. It is possible that he does doubt his virility and masculinity — help him not to. Make sure that you are available for your husband to share his deepest thoughts with you. Help him to feel that he is safe when he confides in you and that you will not judge him. Help him to know that you accept him unconditionally and then he will feel able to share the tumultuous thoughts and doubts in his mind. Never make him feel silly and don't squash his ideas. Remember that this storm has to be ridden out; and once you are through it, life will return to the calm you used to know.

Women and mums

For many women the crisis time has come a few years earlier, at about the age of thirty five. A wife and mother cannot escape the realisation that her children are growing up, that they will soon have left home, and she will be left with an empty house and little purpose to life. A life that revolved around her family has lost its central focus. It seems monotonous and dull. You are still needed as a mother, apparently your family cannot survive without you, but your days are so boring that you cannot see why you are necessary to the family! Everyone leaves for work or school in the early morning, and you are left with the chores to do all day, until the family returns at night. You begin to feel like a housework-machine. The house is empty all day, and you are alone unless you make an effort to go out and meet people.

You may find yourself examining your life and asking yourself: 'What have I accomplished of lasting value in all those years that have passed?' You look at your children and are only partly satisfied with your record in bringing them up. You ask yourself another more searching question: 'What have I as an individual contributed to the world?' The answer, 'Two children' does not satisfy you. 'Surely', you reason, 'there is more to life than this.' You look at your husband and see him still climbing his career ladder. You look at your children about to head off on their independent paths. You look at yourself with life now one-half over, and so little to show for it. And no wonder your peace of mind evaporates. You may resent being an unpaid servant in your family. But you may feel guilty for admitting this to yourself, because you know that as a Christian you should be willing to serve others — and that includes your family as much as anyone else.

Husbands, you can help your wife if you encourage your growing children to help around the house; first setting an example yourself! Help her to know that none of you take her for granted. If she wants to take up activities, or to work outside the home then don't hinder her unless there is a very good reason for doing so. She is going to have to find a new place and role in life when her years of mothering are over and she may need to prepare for this now.

Reinforcing your marriage

If the most important gift you can give your children is a stable, close marriage then you will have to work hard at your marriage in mid-life. The 'being in love' stage has passed, and you will probably have reached a comfortable sense of togetherness and a quiet love. There is a lot you can do to strengthen your marriage, and to get it out of the rut into which it may have fallen.

As marriage partners learn to put out antennae so that you are extra sensitive to one another. Make time to talk and to share the things that really matter to both of you. A husband will help his wife if he remembers to affirm her sexually and vice versa. That means taking time to make love even when life is busy, and routine envelops everything. It also means creatively and imaginatively letting your wife know that she is still sexually attractive to you. This can cost as little as picking a single red rose from the garden, and giving it to her with a card bearing a special message of love. It can cost as much as taking her away for a second or seventeenth honeymoon; when the two of you alone together, rediscover the joy you can have in one another.

Falling in love at forty
Both men and women need to be wary at this age. Both may be in danger of slipping into too close a relationship with someone of the opposite sex without realizing what is happening. This may arise from the need for emotional satisfaction that is no longer supplied by a marriage partner, or it may come from the need for sexual affirmation, or from a vague sense that life is slipping by and opportunities should no longer be passed over. It is said that Christian marriages sometimes suffer here due to a failure to work at marriage. God did not design marriage to be like that.

If this happens to you then you can be sure that your teenagers will notice even though you think you have concealed it perfectly. Any cooling off in the love that existed between you and your partner is sensed. If you are having an extra-marital affair then you must think seriously of the terrible repercussions its discovery would have on your teenagers. They could be shattered by it, and stable foundations whipped away from under their feet. Sadly, parents are most vulnerable to these temptations at the time when teenagers need parent's marriages to be as secure and stable as possible.

It is easier to be wise after an event then before. Don't claim that you are immune to such temptations because you go to church and belong to a Christian family. You are human, and therefore part of fallen humanity, and even you could fall into this trap. To fall in love with someone at forty is painfully beautiful; like something you have never experienced before, and something you know will never be so sweet again. Be on guard against this. If you have a relationship with someone that is closer than you sense it should be for your family's sake, then you will need to be ruthless and terminate it. Try not to let yourself fall in love with someone else at forty!

Cold war marriages

If you face friction as a couple you can be sure that your children will have sensed it. If you have had a blazing row then of course they have heard you. They also sense the battles of a cold war in a marriage. Don't hide the other side of the coin from them. They need the reassurance of knowing that after a row you turn to one another and renew your love in one another's arms. Don't deny them the reassurance of knowing this by hiding under a cloak of unbiblical prudery. Hint (in a way that they will understand) that you love each other enough to make love after rows. Your teenager needs this reassurance but he does not need embarrassing explanations!

As a couple you may need to reassess your marriage frankly and penetratingly, and re-commit yourselves to one another. Marriages often go stale at this time. The husband is at his peak professionally, and work may demand more than he can give. Because of your experience you probably find that your church is demanding time and energy. Home life may be squeezed out in the face of other demands. Little time may be available for your marriage; and any relationship withers if it is allowed to lie dormant and uncultivated. You cannot put your marriage into cold storage and say: 'When life calms down and things get quieter, and I'm not so tired then I'll have time for my marriage', or you may not have a marriage left to have time for.

Your vulnerability

Your teenagers will be watching and sensing what is going on. They observe their parents struggling within themselves. Hopefully, they see you as a couple aiming to put things right. As they watch they will learn lessons that are invaluable for their handling of their own relationships, later on in adult life. You will probably be especially vulnerable to any criticism your teenager levels

67

at you. His apparent lack of tolerance and impatience may hurt you. You may possibly feel ashamed of the doubts and questions that flood unbidden and unwanted to your mind. You may find it virtually impossible to be honest in your answers to your teenager's questions about your Christianity if you think through your faith again for yourself. You may wonder how you can possibly help your child spiritually if you face doubts and questions similar to his. Your child will respect you for honest questions and doubts: but you may feel it wiser at this stage to keep them to yourself until you have sorted them out. It is true, but of little comfort to you at this time, that most people question at some time even their deepest religious beliefs. And the majority emerge at the other end of this reassessment with a faith that is more solid and richer than ever before.

Your insecure teenager needs to feel safe in the strength of your marriage. So, try not to let mid-life crises hit you unawares, thus giving your teenager shaky ground under his feet. A loving marriage relationship is deepened and strengthened by the testing years of mid-life crises.

Church commitments

If the greatest gift you can give your children is a strong marriage aim to make sure it is at its strongest at this stage of life. 'I can't . . .' you may respond, 'there are all the committees I'm on, the meetings I lead, and all the responsibility I have outside home. . . '

God may be asking you to reassess all the things you are doing, and to stop many of them. Sit down and list your out-of-work activities. Then prayerfully ask the hard question: 'What on this list has God specifically told me to do? What am I doing because I assume God wants me to do it but I have never consulted him? And why have I never asked him?' You are likely to find that you are doing far too many things, because you are doing things (good in themselves) that God never intended you to do. In a survey of Christian marriages conducted by

Family magazine in 1980, the major cause of stress located in Christian marriages was 'too many church commitments'. If your marriage is under stress for this reason then the stress in your marriage will have repercussions on your children. I am convinced that many Christian parents accept too much church responsibility without first finding out whether God wants them to carry it or not.

I am also sure that during your children's formative years God intends you to be available to them. That does not mean that you neglect your role in your church but rather that you extra prayerfully try to see what God (not the minister) intends that role to be while your children still need you.

Accepting your failures

You may look at your marriage and at your children, and decide that you are a failure. You may think that you are to blame for everything your teenager does 'wrong'. You may assume a whole load of guilt that was not there before. If you feel a failure as a marriage partner or as a parent, then don't wallow in it. God does not intend you to remain in gloom. Find somewhere quiet to think alone, or go and share your thoughts with a Christian you trust. Then bring your burden of guilt and failure to God. Bring it to Jesus' cross — and accept the forgiveness that he wants you to receive from him. It doesn't matter what you've done (or not done), God's loving mercy is there for you. God waits for you to accept his forgiveness and, like Pilgrim, to roll your burden off at the foot of the cross. He does not intend you to pick up that load and stagger off with it again! Leave it there. As God has forgiven so you must learn to forget — and you must learn to accept yourself as a 'failed' parent if necessary, because God does.

This is a stage of new beginnings. You start off again on a new phase of life with fresh commitments to your marriage partner, to your children and to God. As you do this you are better able to help your teenagers. And they appreciate the fact that you, being human like them, know what it is like to doubt, to fear, and to go on walking forwards despite the uncertain darkness of the path.

7: What is home?

'Home . . . ' her deep eyes were wistful and her voice thoughtful, 'I didn't know how much I appreciated home until I went off to college. . . '

'Funny thing that', I mused, 'I always thought you longed to break free from your family and be independent'.

'So did I', she confessed.

Unconditional love

Home, to your teenager, should be the one place in the world where he feels most comfortable, most at peace and most free to be his real self. And this is supremely true when your teenager feels safe enough at home to be at his worst with you. There is one sense in which you can accept this behaviour as a compliment, because your teenager must know that you accept him if he is able to be his worst at home.

Your teenager needs to know that you love him unconditionally. He needs to be able to express feelings he dare not show elsewhere, in case he is rejected. He needs the assurance that you love him whether he is nice or nasty; and when he makes life difficult for himself and everyone else he may simply be testing your love to see if it fails under pressure.

Your teenager will go through phases (and the degree varies with different people) of rejecting and hating himself. He will go through stages of feeling a total failure, and very inadequate as a person. At home he needs to know that he not only belongs, but that he is accepted regardless of the kind of person he is. He needs to know that he does not have to conform to a certain type of person but that you love him for his hidden qualities and the real self he is discovering himself to be.

Open house

'Love me love my dog', says one kind of person. Perhaps your teenager wants to say something vaguely similar but something you would rather not hear: 'Love me, love my friends . . . ' This is not the time to swallow hard and back away nervously. If you dislike his friends then your teenager will probably know this already, because you (like most parents) will at some time or other have told him so.

It is very important for you to build relationships with your teenager's friends. It is also important for you to have the kind of atmosphere at home into which your children feel able to bring their friends. It is their home as well as yours (isn't it?). You may need to brace yourself and be ready for disruption of the house. The disadvantages of disruption are far outweighed by the benefits all of you will gain from this. Get ready for the music that will almost inevitably start up when your teenager entertains, and try not to ask for it to be turned down unless you are on the point of losing all your neighbours, or granny is about to have another stroke. Watch yourself while his friends are in your home; you could do all kinds of things that would cause embarrassment. Make sure, if you can, that you are well stocked up with food, so that the advent of your teenager's friends does not necessarily disorganise next week's meals. A few teenage boys are capable of leaving a fridge looking as if a swarm of locusts have passed through it. Stock up well and be prepared. If transport home at night is a problem for his friends, then you may be needed to act as a kind of free taxi service. Your teenager may be relieved if you offer to do this, and also if you make the telephone available for his friends to 'phone home to say if they are going to be later than expected.

Family finances

As your teenager increasingly learns that his home really is his home, as well as yours, he must learn how to carry part of the responsibility for running it. A major area of learning that may come as a nasty shock to him is in the area of family finances, or the lack of them. If you are preparing him to live in the real world (as you should be) then you need to help him understand about family finance, so that when he leaves home and is independent he does not have to handle finances for the first time.

I see no reason why a teenager should not understand how family finances work. Sit down together and explain how much comes in from each different source. Then explain what goes out and where it goes. He needs to understand about fixed outgoings that have to be paid regardless every momth (mortgage, insurance and so on) and then to understand how you allocate the rest of your family income. This can be useful for you as well as for your teenager. You will find that you are questioned about some bills, and about the wisdom of using money in certain ways. Your children may see your family finances in a different light from you, and you may find that as you listen to them you have to agree that they are right. You may change some of your patterns of spending in line with their suggestions. As no parents are expected to be all knowing or all powerful there is nothing wrong in this. You may need to be extra humble about a matter that your own parents' generation probably regarded as private and not open to discussion or criticism within the family. You need not feel threatened by your teenager's criticisms or suggestions. Be grateful instead that God may be teaching you lessons through your family that he cannot show you in any other way.

'Why do we have baths?' Janet asked her mother.

The reply was simple: 'To be clean . . . '

Janet persisted, 'But it's cheaper to have showers . . . and if we are trying not to live extravagantly then why don't we have a shower fitted?'

Her parents had never thought about this; a good idea

73

which fitted into the simple life style they wanted to adopt.

Depending on God

As you share family finances never let your children be worried about money. Try to help them to understand that the God of the Bible, the God who has told us not to worry about these things, is looking after you and your family. He will never let you or your children go without things you really need. Try to share frankly the times that you have been at financial rock-bottom, and the ways in which God helped you out. This will give your children a very secure foundation to their lives as adults. Adults who are able to rest in the assurance that God will never let them down financially are adults whose faith is rock solid and can stand life's storms.

Learn to pray with your children about money when they are tiny, so that when they are teenagers this will be a natural pattern for your family life. Teach your children that God is concerned about new socks for the toddler, about food for the cat, about maintenance of the car, about the family holiday, and about the very big things like buying a house. As you talk about family finances together, your teenager ought to see that family money is being used fairly and wisely. He ought to see that you are trying to use money as God wants you to. If it seems unfair, then try and explain the reasons to him. Open discussion of total family finances helps him to get his pocket money into perspective and to see where it fits into overall family budgeting. His parents' purse stops being an Aladdin's lamp.

Making allowances

You may find it helpful to give your teenager an annual allowance out of which he is expected to buy all his clothes. Families vary enormously in their practice here. Some teenagers are not ready to manage their own money to this extent, and other families cannot afford to give their teenagers a fixed allowance. If you can do this, then you will be giving your teenager valuable lessons in learning how to manage money on his own. He will make mistakes, and you may or may not feel you should come to the rescue with your hand in your wallet. At the very least, he will learn that once he has spent his money it is all gone: a salutary lesson everyone must discover at some time or another.

Once your teenager starts to earn real money then it will help him to learn how to spend real money in real ways. You may not want to ask for board and lodging money from him when he starts his first job, but it is still sensible to ask for a realistic sum weekly. He will then learn how to budget for himself and how to work out a pattern of living that is within his means. Some parents invest the money they have received from their children, and return it later as a surprise present. Whether or not your teenager does a Saturday job, holiday jobs, or morning paper rounds will depend on you, your teenager, and the availability of jobs where you live. Some teenagers grow tired if they do outside jobs, and school work suffers. Others gain from the small financial independence such jobs afford. You know your teenager better than anyone else and you are the best person to help him think this through sensibly. But give him the opportunity to learn how to carry his part of the responsibility in running your home.

Families are different, and so you cannot compare the way you do things with the way other families function. Into this category put the vexed question of whether or not you pay a teenager for the work he does around the house. Some parents want to teach their children that they are responsible members of a family unit, and that a working mother should not have to come home and be expected to do all the housework, while the rest of the family sits slumped round the television. Other families will feel that work done at home is as worthy of payment as work outside the home: and that if a teenager does a job that someone else would have been paid to do then the teenager should receive payment. If you are paying your teenagers then find out the going-rate in your area for the jobs that are being done. Pay fairly, unless you and your child agree that to help family budgeting you will pay less. Do not be stingy but equally do not be over-generous.

As Christians you will be aiming at a simple life style which is consistent with Jesus' teaching as you understand it. Do not encourage your children to be caught in the web of today's materialistic society. The place where your children learn about life style is at home. It is at home that they see whether or not you are keeping up with the Jones's. If next door has a new coat of paint when the old one is still acceptable, and if next door has hundreds of the latest gadgets then your children will be watching to see whethere you try to conform or not. They will respect you if you give your reasons for opting out of the materialistic rat-race. But it is necessary for you to give reasons for what you do to avoid misinterpretation.

Tight budgets

Some children feel humiliated if their parents have less money than other parents. Try and understand your teenager and know how he feels about you. He may not be bothered but he may be resentful if you lack resources. If you are a full-time Christian worker (children of ministers and missionaries come into this category) then he may resent the fact that you earn little. The fact that God always supplies what you all need may not mean a great deal to your teenager right now. He may be ashamed that you do not get a good day's pay for a good day's work (and he may even wonder if you are doing a good day's work, or if you are not worth paying properly).

Do not run away from this problem if your child is facing it. The resentment and bitterness he may carry needs handling sensitively or it may turn to bitterness against a church that apparently fails to support its workers, and even into a rejection of the God of such a church. This is the last thing you want your teenager to experience. Bring the subject out into the open. Discuss how you all feel about having less in the way of financial resources than others. Discuss different ways of coping financially. Find out how each one of you reacts to buying clothes in nearly-new shops or at jumble sales. If you are a full-time Christian worker, and your children resent your low income, you may fear to bring the subject out into the open in case this results in you offering to leave your calling for secular work, because of pressure from children. I do not think God wants you to fear this. I anticipate you will find that your teenagers respect you for letting them share in the problem. They will respect you for having brought them in, and for not having been excluded in something that closely involves them. In the end you are likely to find that your teenagers rally in support of you and your calling. You may even find that your entire family wants to pledge itself to be part of God's calling to you. Your family will pull together to make it possible for you to do this job.

This may necessitate mother working outside the home, and teenagers doing odd jobs around the house at weekends for no payment. It may involve stringent family economies. If the family is working together to free one, or both, parents for the task to which God has called them, this can be a source of tremendous strength to a family. In the end your children will receive far more blessing than they have ever given and their efforts and sacrifices will be repaid one hundredfold.

Giving to God
When you share principles underlying the handling of your family finances you will want to explain to your teenagers about giving money to God. You may feel odd about doing this, and recall the Bible words about 'not letting your left hand know what your right hand does'. Remember that the money you give to God out of the family bank account is in fact family money (unless you regard all money as your own personal money, in which

case you will have a different outlook on family finances from me).

You may find that your teenagers are relieved to hear that you do give a regular percentage of your income to God's work. They may have been more bothered about this than you realised. They may not have known that you were giving to missions and to the third world (and how could they know if you did not tell them). If you covenant your money then use this as an opportunity to teach them about the benefits of covenanting. You may face some surprises: like the teenager who thought his parents only gave God the 10 pence he saw dropped into the collection plate every Sunday, and never knew of the £50 that went to the church through standing order with the bank as part of a covenant.

Running the home

Home is your teenager's home as well as yours. The older he gets the more he will be able to appreciate the fact that a home needs looking after, and that it is right and fair for him to share in what needs doing to keep a home running. If you are sharing routine housework as a family then make sure that it is shared out fairly. Do not always give the worst jobs to the family member who will complain least, in the end he will notice and resent this fact. And you will be teaching the rest of the family that unwillingness to help pays!

Make sure that everyone does their fair share, and that the same person doesn't skive every time — most families have a skiver! You may not like the thought of a frontal encounter with the 'offender' to get him to carry his full share. It is probably easier for you silently to get on and do what he has left undone. Yet, in the end this is not fair on the rest of the family and certainly does not help the one involved.

Your teenagers will expect you to run the house, and will not expect (or even think) of thanking you for this. Parents are there to look after their children, or so they unthinkingly assume. Yet your teenager will expect you to be lavish in praise and gratitude for a job well done by him at home. Not only does he deserve thanks but he will need this recognition and affirmation of himself as a person. Make sure that when your teenagers help in the house they don't have to do the most boring jobs. Let them do the jobs that are creative and fun if there is any choice. Try and do the dull ones yourself: you'll survive better! If dad takes on the heavy, messy and boring jobs then children are learning by seeing that wives and mothers are not servants. This is a valuable lesson for adult life. In all this remember that your teenager is working towards adult independence. Life may seem to be a round of arguments about who washes-up which meals, but underneath lies more than washing-up. The oldest teenager may feel that the youngest child is let off too lightly and gets away with helping too little. Yet he may be expressing far more than his feelings about washing-up in what he says about housework — he may really be trying to communicate his problems in accepting the responsibility he shoulders as the oldest child. Listen and hear what he is saying under the words he actually speaks.

Home should be home to your teenager. Somewhere he belongs, somewhere where he learns about family life, and somewhere where he can bring his friends and know that they, as well as he, will find unconditional acceptance.

8: Sex in a secular society

'My teenagers are growing up in a world that's totally different from the one which I grew up in . . . ' she said. And she is certainly not the first mother to make a statement like that. Nor is she the first parent to be perplexed by what is going on in her child's life. Nowhere have basic assumptions, attitudes and teachings changed more in the last ten to twenty years, than in the area of moral and sexual standards.

Pressures of permissiveness

In 1981 a leading weekly woman's magazine carried out a survey among its readers. The results showed that three out of every four women who responded to the questionnaire felt that today's teenagers are under too much pressure to have sexual intercourse before marriage. Over half the girls under twenty who replied agreed with this. They said that permissiveness has been allowed to go too far. Nearly half believed that sixteen is the right legal age of consent for girls but one-third felt that young people should be protected under stricter laws and that the current laws should be scrapped. When a popular weekly woman's magazine publishes survey results saying that sexual permissiveness has gone too far, then you can argue with those who claim that a church which has the same view is 'old fashioned and irrelevant'. Christians should listen and learn from results like these.

One of the questions at the heart of the sexual permissiveness problem is: 'Who is responsible for teaching children about sexuality?' The womans' magazine survey answered, '78 per cent said that this should be shared between parents and schools'. I suppose that in our modern world such a reaction is reasonable, and that there are many good reasons why schools should teach about sexuality. Apparently many parents do not do this, and children are left untaught in one of life's most important areas. I believe that Christian parents have a responsibility not only to teach their children all the 'facts of life' themselves but also to impart Christian standards of behaviour. I am convinced that they should not leave this to other people. If your children are going to understand Christian standards then you must teach your children yourselves. This is a responsibility you cannot delegate to others.

Whether doctors and clinics which provide contraceptives to girls under the age of 16 (that is under the legal age of consent) should inform the girl's parents or not is another hotly disputed question. In the woman's magazine survey about 64 per cent of those replying believed that by providing contraception to teenagers under the age of 16, unwanted pregnancies would be avoided. Only about 34 per cent stated that they thought this encouraged sexual activity in teenagers who were under age.

If all this had been debated when you were a teenager then you would be better equipped to understand what your children face today. Possibly you are old enough to have heard about contraception first of all when you were planning to get married. And then it was discussed in hushed tones behind closed doors; it probably was not taught in class in your school as it is today.

Parents — your crucial role
What has happened? Why have things changed? One reason is that we now live in what some people call a 'post-Christian era'. The Christian standards that were accepted as normal in the past are now questioned, and many have been discarded. Another reason is that we live in a so-called 'pluralistic society'. This results in

educators upholding the values of different religions and philosophies, and deciding that different viewpoints must be presented fairly in schools. The Christian standard is no longer accepted as either normal or best.

This means that Christian parents play a crucial role in teaching their children Christian standards. Your children may receive teaching based on Christian standards at school but there is no guarantee of this. Unless you teach your children yourself they may not hear Christian values. Valuable as church youth activities are, these cannot take the place of teaching Christian sexual standards at home. Never leave this to school or to church youth groups. It is your own responsibility and no one else's.

It is easy to slip into assuming that the welfare state is a kind of super-parent both to you and to your family. The welfare state cares for you when you are ill, looks after you in old age, and now even tries to ensure that your teenagers do not get pregnant under-age! This would be fine provided the welfare state — this super-parent — made sure that Christian ethical standards were upheld. But there is no reason why it should — it is there to cater for all people of all religious persuasions.

Government concern

Recently, facts have emerged that have caused the government to take action about what is happening to today's teenagers. By the Autumn of 1981, government concern about teenager sexual activity was such that it funded the Health Education Council, to launch a campaign aimed at teenagers, specifically designed to motivate them to seek contraceptive help and advice. Sir George Young, the junior health minister, stated in 1981 that the government wanted to reassert traditional family values, and that the decision to give advice on birth control to young teenagers, and to make contraceptive advice freely available to unmarried young people was controversial. He said: 'But to attempt to restore family values by the wholesale curtailment of availability of

82

contraceptive advice to young people would, in my view, be an irresponsible blind act of faith. The government thought that it should be only under exceptional circumstances that girls under 16 should be given contraceptives without their parents' knowledge'.

He continued: 'We realise that this makes the job of doctors and other professionals dealing with under 16's very difficult. Trying to persuade a girl to involve her parents could well turn her away from the very sources of help that might prevent an unplanned pregnancy. . . . Although it is my strong view that parents should be involved normally, I want to make it clear that ultimately the decision whether or not to prescribe contraceptives without reference to parents must be for individual doctors and, in exceptional cases, the doctor may decide not to inform the parents'.

He added: 'I consider it necessary that any material for this age group makes it clear that the option of chastity is not a vestigial concept of the 19th century but something that has relevance for today'.

Appalling facts
The government is concerned because in 1981 teenage abortions increased and more unmarried girls under the age of 20 had abortions than ever before. In 1979, 33,000 unmarried teenagers had legal abortions and by 1981, the rate was still rising. The number of unmarried teenage mothers has also increased since 1977, with the top figure of 24,000 being reached in 1979.

So, the government is right to be concerned, and is acting responsibly in trying to stop teenage abortions and pregnancies. It is an unpalatable fact that parents may have to accept that teenagers are going to experiment sexually, especially in today's culture, and that they need to be taught how not to get pregnant.

Teach teenagers 'no'
However, I am convinced that Christian parents must go much further back than this. Teaching contraception is

correcting a symptom of a disease: we must eradicate the disease and prevent the symptoms from ever occuring. We must teach teenagers that the best way of not getting pregnant is not to have sexual intercourse. We must help them to understand that the word 'no' is better than any pill or sheath. There are good reasons for avoiding sexual intercourse outside marriage both for physical and for psychiatric reasons. I believe that these reasons lie behind the teaching of the Bible that intercourse was designed by God for marriage only, and that in God's plan he made man and woman to function most perfectly when it is within the framework of 'one man, one woman, for life'. God was not acting as a kill-joy. He did not design us like this to stop us from having fun. He made us like this so that we would derive the maximum delight and enrichment from one of the most precious gifts he gave mankind.

Your teenager may have picked up the idea that sex outside marriage is fun and harmless. You must teach him the joy and fulfilment of sex within marriage and that it can be harmful outside marriage. He needs to know the risks of venereal disease, and that a girl can be rendered infertile if she contracts VD. He also needs to know that promiscuity increases the risk of a certain form of cancer of the mouth of the womb in young people. He must be alerted to the possible psychiatric repercussions of sexual intercourse outside marriage. It may be called 'sex for fun' but it is fun for which a heavy price is often paid — a price he might prefer not to pay had you warned him of the risks.

Today's society has discarded Christian standards and values. It claims that there are no such things as moral absolutes. Many people find it odd and old-fashioned that the church should say 'no' to intercourse outside marriage. Many people have been influenced by 'situational ethics'. This is a form of teaching that there are no absolute standards of what is right and what is wrong. The view taken in simple terms is that if something feels good, and if you want to do it, then it is all right to do it — as long as no one gets hurt in the process. This cuts right across biblical teaching that certain things are right and others are wrong. As a Christian I believe that there are moral absolutes, and reject all teaching that claims there are none.

Your teenager is growing up in this kind of society. He is facing a world whose standards of sexual morality are different from those you hold. If you find a packet of contraceptive pills under your daughter's mattress, or a contraceptive sheath in your son's pocket, then you will understand first-hand the extent to which modern society has influenced your own children.

Giving support

It is likely that your teenager will learn about contraceptives in class at school. You do not have the legal right to withdraw him from sex education (which is part of the syllabus of a wide variety of subjects and not just biology). But you do have a legal right to withdraw your child from any religious education that you find unacceptable.

Go and talk to your child's Headmaster about the content of a syllabus and your reaction to it, if it concerns you. This is part of your responsibility both to your child and to other children. The Head is the person who decides who will give sex education in his school, and he is ultimately responsible for what is taught and for the way in which it is taught. If you discover something that is morally unacceptable to you or something you find offensive then go and share this politely with him. Beware of conveying the impression that you are more of a religious fanatic than you really are, or that you are one of those parents who are trouble-makers. Be polite and considerate, and remember that the Head is doing what he thinks is best for as many of the children in the school as he possibly can. Help him to know that he has your support in other matters, if not in the sex education which may be given outside a Christian framework.

Your children need a positive lead at home to counteract what they are learning from magazines, books, films, tv, and perhaps school. Help your child to understand that 'no' is the best way of stopping unwanted pregnancies, and that to say 'no' is not to deny virility or femininity. He will need courage if he has to stand out and be different from his friends, and perhaps say, 'I have to be different . . . that is wrong.'

What sex is all about
By the time your children are teenagers you ought to have taught them the basics of sex education. Hopefully they will have learned this from you and not from biology lessons, or smutty stories at school. Your children should have learned from you when they were little that there is more to sexual intercourse than the mating of male and female.

You must communicate to your children what sex is all about; and this will be much easier if you have started doing this virtually since each child was born. You may find it difficult. If so, it is possible that God is asking you to let go of your inhibitions, for the sake of your teenager, and to have the courage to talk openly.

A few weeks ago a group of teenagers shared their reactions about their parents with me. 'I couldn't possibly talk to them about sex,' was the consensus of opinion, 'they are far too embarrassed. . .'

Embarrassment about sex
Many parents let their children down by being unwilling to talk about sex: one subject that teenagers usually discuss freely among themselves. If you find the subject difficult and embarrassing then the best way to start is to begin by talking to your marriage partner about your own sexual relationship. If you are unable to talk to your children, then it is possible and even likely that you are not talking to one another about it. Break down one communication barrier by talking to each other. After all, this is an area of life that you share together, and it is vital for you to discuss it with each another. Once you

have done so, you will find that it is far less embarrassing than you imagined it would be. Talking to your marriage partner can be the first step towards talking to your teenagers.

You must break this communication barrier for the sake of your children or they will never learn what you, and you alone, should be teaching them. How can they learn about sexuality from a Christian viewpoint if you are not teaching them? It should hardly surprise or shock you if you find that they adopt non-Christian standards, if at home they hear nothing on this vital matter.

I remember the boy who stated categorically: 'My parents never taught us anything about sex. . . ' And his parents, in a separate interview, said: 'We never made a special thing out of teaching our children about sex . . . we tried to make it a natural and normal part of life so that it wasn't something separate or different. We tried to talk about it in the same way that we talk about anything else. . . ' And the end result? Their son claimed that he was never taught about sex. It was an integrated part of his parents' approach to life, and yet he had never been lectured on the subject — but then he had never been lectured on other subjects basic to daily living.

Somehow you are going to have to teach your children in a way that does not sound pious, legalistic or joyless. Christians tend to sound just like that when talking about sex. Sexual intercourse was given by God when he created the world, as one of his most precious, and most joy-filled gifts. It was something that God intended man to enjoy. It is precisely this that you must communicate to your children. You must teach them how to enjoy this gift without misusing and so spoiling it.

Spotlight on you

The way your children will learn the most is through you. And the quality of relationship that you have as a married couple will mean far more to your teenagers than anything you say to them. They will sense the quality of your sexual relationship (its richness or its poverty) without you needing to explain in detail to them. This puts the spotlight of teaching about sex on your own personal life.

You cannot expect your child to learn what God intended, if you do not live it at home. And this may be the area in which you can help him more than you realise. So, sort out this part of your life if necessary. If you have run into trouble sexually as a married couple, and you are unable to work things out together, then get help without hesitating. You will be helping your teenager as well as yourselves, making it doubly important.

As a couple you cannot be making passes at one another all the time. But try not to limit your expressions of affection for one another to times when your children are out of the room. They will sense the assurance that you do love one another. They will see that you are sexually satisfying to each other, and that neither partner has a need to flirt with anyone else. This is seen and learned more powerfully by action rather than by embarrassed talk.

'Mum', Sheila was a vivacious eighteen year old, out to enjoy all that life offered her, 'Don't you and dad find one another boring? After all you've been married twenty years. . .'

In reply to her mother's puzzled silence, she continued, 'Do you know, I find you two almost embarrassing. You're the only couple I know who've never slept with anyone else. . .' But her tone of voice indicated that not only did she approve but she wanted love to turn out like that for her too.

Your children are your responsibility. The State has to step in if you are not doing your job, but I believe that every Christian parent has the God-given responsibility not to abdicate this responsibility to the welfare state.

9: Learning to love

'I wish my parents could talk about sex the way you do to me. . .' Peter said to me recently.

'How do you mean?' I asked. I didn't think that I had said anything exceptional.

He continued, 'What you said makes sense'.

I was relieved but I was also sad because I had said nothing that Peter's parents could not have explained to him themselves.

Sexual differences

It will help your teenagers if you can help them understand the difference in the thinking and emotional reactions of men and women. Unless you teach them they may never know or — what is worse — they may pick up half-truths or wrong ideas from sources that you would prefer them to avoid.

For instance, your teenage son won't tell you, but as he is developing he will find that he is sexually aroused by the sight of a girl's body, by her looks and even by her words. He is quickly aroused, especially by sight. Your daughter functions differently. Sexual awakening usually comes for her in the context of a relationship. As she gets to know a boy (or a man), so a relationship of trust and friendship develops, and within the context of this relationship she becomes ready for sexual arousal. His touch, kiss or caress will awaken that which is dormant within her. This happens more slowly for a young woman but it happens at a far deeper level than for a young man.

Sexual intercourse satisfies a man quickly and immediately. Usually a woman responds more slowly, and is frustrated if her partner has been too quick for her.

When a woman gives herself to a man she is giving the man far more than just her body. She usually is giving him her whole self in love. If he then leaves her she may be hurt deeply. For some women an experience like this leaves scars that may lead to an inability to respond fully to the man who later becomes her husband. This is one reason why 'one night stands', or short affairs, can be psychologically harmful to a girl. Casual sex, early in life, may lead to an inability to develop a deep and meaningful relationship in an exclusive marriage bond later on.

Your teenagers need to understand that they pay what I regard as an exorbitant price for casual sex. They should also be aware that few couples experience the full potential of sexual intercourse if this takes place outside the framework of marriage.

Sleeping together

Many young couples who sleep together before marriage later say that they wish they had never done so. To begin with, they cannot be sure whether or not they are suited as marriage partners just by sleeping together. There is no such thing as 'sexual compatibility'. A man's penis fits a woman's vagina, unless there is something in the woman that needs correcting medically. You cannot experiment with intercourse to see whether or not you 'fit' each other. Intercourse does not work like that. Some couples find that they cannot express their love fully outside the security of the commitment that comes through the marriage bond. This is especially true for girls. Some cannot give themselves totally without the loving commitment that belongs to marriage. Therefore their expression of love is less than it could be, and not all that God designed it to be.

Many married couples need months or years learning how best to fulfil one another sexually. The act itself is simple but learning how best to express love in sexual intercourse is something that takes time. Many couples find that the longer they are married the richer and fuller their sexual life becomes because they know each other better. This is one of the reasons why 'trial marriages' are an inadequate guide as to whether or not a couple are suited as life partners.

If your teenager sleeps with someone before marriage then he may find his judgement is blurred and he is unable to make the right decision about marriage itself. The sexual side of a relationship (once it is allowed to develop and be prominent) may so colour everything that he cannot see the other person clearly and rationally. He may be so infatuated sexually that he does not know the other person as an individual, and is unable to size up whether this person is right as a life partner or not.

You will never be able to deliver a lecture on all this to your teenager, nor should you sit him in a corner and try to! Be ready and know your reasons in case you are asked them. Seize any opportunities that may arise when you are watching tv or talking together. Don't force the issue but don't run away from it if it arises naturally! Your teenager needs the security of knowing that you stand firmly by your Christian ethical standards.

If you do talk at a deep level with your own teenager then you may need to consciously decide to be unshock-able. If your teenagers know that certain things will upset you, then they are unlikely to discuss those things in front of you. If they know that you are not obviously going to be horrified then they may feel able to talk openly in your presence, and you may have the opportunity of saying the things they want you to.

Marriage expectations
You may have heard that today's teenagers have largely given up the idea of marriage as a good thing. You may be reassured to know that in 1981 the *Daily Mail* ported that this 'myth' should be dispelled. One of its surveys indicated that nine out of ten teenagers look forward to their wedding day as one of the biggest days of their

lives. Most girls regarded twenty as the ideal age for marriage, and most teenagers expected to be married with their own families by the time they were twenty five. Marriage is still very fashionable!

However, you may hear your teenager discussing marriage in a way that is different from your idea of it. It will help you to understand some basic changes in thinking about marriage that have occurred in the last twenty years. When your grandparents married they probably regarded marriage as the means to an end — believing that fulfilment in marriage was a great bonus but could not necessarily be expected. You may have assumed your grandparents' outlook without thinking. But today, marriage is seen as an end in itself. Your teenager is likely to believe that when he gets married he has a right to have a fulfilled, compatible and happy marriage. He will probably believe that this is the point of marriage. He may believe that if it fails to provide fulfilment then it is best ended by divorce.

You yourself may not quite know what to think! When you married you were in love, and probably never thought about what you expected from your marriage. As the years passed you may have realised that you must work at it, and that you must stick with your partner. However, in recent years you may have shifted your thinking to bring it in line with modern secular thinking, without realising what was happening to you.

Expectations of a marriage have changed in the last twenty years. You may need to sit down as a couple to re-evaluate your own marriage, and to commit yourselves again to one another. Even as Christians one, or both, of you may unconsciously have come to the conclusion that you can opt out of marriage if it fails to provide fulfilment. Perhaps you are sticking together as a couple just 'until the children are grown up'. If this is so, then sit down and re-consider and pray again about this situation. Even 'grown up' children can be hurt deeply if parents divorce or separate.

Deep relationships

During his late teens your teenager will be assessing the value of marriage. He will be weighing up whether it is for him or not, and if so he will be dreaming of the type of partner for which he is looking. Unconsciously he will be watching you and what he sees gives him a pattern to follow later on when he himself is a marriage partner. You are his model, and this is one reason why you have an important role to play in your child's life in the quality of married life you demonstrate to him. By watching you, he learns how to be a Christian husband and father, or wife and mother. Your example will be carried through to the next generation by your children.

One of the important lessons you can teach your child is how to form deep relationships with other people. This is something that is deeper than sexual intimacy. It involves being safe enough with another person to dare to expose the depths of your thoughts and emotions, where you are most vulnerable to being hurt. If your teenagers see you risking exposing yourselves to each other then they will know that this is safe for them. On the other hand, they may learn from you that it is not safe to share your real self — for fear of hurt — and that it is safer to stay in a shell. They may learn not to share their feelings with another person. Probably this has never been stated, nor has any reason been given for it. They see that you do not do it, and so they do not share themselves deeply with friends either. And so a closed isolation of personality is carried down from one generation to another.

Women today

At home, your teenager also begins to work out his attitude towards the changing role of women in today's society. You will show him Jesus' attitude towards women by yours, or you may give him the wrong impression. It is important for you to think this through as a married couple. Your teenager is moving in a society in which many more women work outside the home than

93

when you were first married. Your children need a clear Christian perspective on this. They need to learn how to treat women. In these days of women's 'lib' should women be treated as equal to men or not? If there are differences, then what are they? Are wives to be expected to do all the housework, as well as a full-time job outside the home or not? How dad does, or does not, help at home will shape your teenager's attitudes towards the place of women in society. Is it unmanly for dad to iron, cook, and help with the housework? If he thinks that it is unmasculine then it is likely that his sons will grow up sharing the same feeling.

If it is Christian to help the wife and mother, then perhaps father needs to learn some basic skills, so that his boys can help their wives in their turn. The Bible urges husbands to love their wives as they love their own bodies. This needs to be applied to each family in the way in which work loads are allocated.

Testing friendships

In early adolescence your teenager will develop close friendships with people of his own age and sex. He will probably be able to share himself and to confide in such friends. This sharing is important for him as he is probably naturally reticent of revealing himself in case he faces rejection. Gradually he will begin to develop friendships with the opposite sex and he is unlikely to consult you about them. When he begins to go out with someone of the opposite sex then pray hard and don't panic. Boy-girl relationships blossom whether parents approve or not. It is now that all the groundwork of what you have taught your teenager since childhood bears fruit. Your teenager is likely to respond to your trust in him more than anything else. Trust counts far more than authority and the knowledge that you trust him to act as you have taught him is a strong factor influencing the way he behaves. However, if he is rebelling against you then he may rebel in his sexual activity. He may feel he has to try out the opposite of what he knows you believe is right. He may do this to prove that he is independent, or else to test you out to see if you are right or wrong, or even to see whether your love stands the stress of him acting in a way that he knows will cause you maximum distress.

First love

This is the time when it is likely that your teenager will fall in love for the first time. Be gentle about this. Remember your own first love, and how fragile it was. First love is unbelievably idealistic. There is no need for you to shatter any illusions your teenager has about his 'beloved' — time will do that for him without your help. For many teenagers sexual attraction does not enter into this first love, which can be a totally self-giving love. It's the kind of love in which your teenager is satisfied if he can just carry his 'beloved's' books. He wants to give, to give and to give again for nothing in return. The sight of his 'beloved' is enough. Sexual desire, on the other hand, involves a degree of selfishness (I want something from another person that will satisfy me) that is missing in an adolescent first love.

Your teenager will see his loved one as perfect and endowed with all kinds of qualities that you cannot see, no matter how carefully you look. No matter how much you want to laugh and tease about this love, you must restrain yourself. You will hurt your teenager badly if you turn this into one of your family jokes — it is not a joke to him. It is very serious, and an important part of growing up. The more successfully your teenager can negotiate this adolescent first love, the more successful he will be at moving onto the next stage of love; the stage in which he finds a serious and lasting love that can progress into marriage. If your teenager wants to bring his boy/girlfriend home with him, then make it easy. Home is the ideal situation in which they can get to know one another, unlike the artificial situations outside home. Try to give the couple as much privacy as possible — you can always say you are tired and go to bed early. You will probably find that the trust your teenager knows you have in him will deter him from acting at home in a way he knows would grieve you.

If your teenager wants to have parties in your house then you are going to have to handle the situation carefully and tactfully. Only you can discern what a 'party' means. In some places it is a harmless getting together with music, and in other areas it involves drink, and perhaps drugs. Only you can decide what should go on in your house. If there is a party in your home then it is a good idea to be around, at least for the later part of the evening. The presence of a parent deters trouble, and your teenager may secretly be very grateful for you to be there if a situation arises which he is unable to control.

10: Guilty feelings about sexuality

'You're the woman who says that all my problems are "normal"!' he said with an engaging smile, over lunch at a youth conference.

I was taken aback for a few seconds. Then recovering my composure, I commented, 'Don't carry a load of guilt around with you that God never intended you to have'.

That young man is like too many teenagers from Christian families who have inherited a burden of guilt from things parents have or have not said. In this particular case the teenager was referring to sexual guilt, but I have talked with others who feel guilty about other things. To the extent of one from a Christian home who stated, 'I feel guilty. . . .'

'What about?' I asked.

'I don't even know . . . that's the trouble . . .' he replied.

You may find that, as a parent, you have to make a definite effort to ensure that your child does not feel guilty for his sexuality, and for the things that happen to him as he develops sexually. Unless you specifically make it possible for him to open some of these areas of his life and talk to you about them he may feel confused about what is happening and be left without help.

'Unforgiveable' sins

Your teenage son is unlikely to mention wet dreams to you. It is possible with his Christian upbringing that he feels that these are something very bad and even sinful. He may not know exactly why they should be bad; he may just sense that they are. He may feel guilty about the sexual fantasies that often accompany wet dreams, and come unbidden into his mind while he is asleep. You are probably going to have to exercise the ultimate in tact to find the right moment to talk to him unemotively about this. Explain that all this is a normal part of growing up, that it is necessary for adult sexual maturity, and that as his body adjusts to all the hormone changes going on this is to be expected. Assure him that eventually wet dreams will stop, when his hormone levels have stabilised.

Neither wet dreams, nor the sexual fantasy that accompanies them while asleep, should be allowed to be a cause of guilt to your teenage son. This is the kind of thing that a vulnerable teenager is likely to fasten onto as 'the unforgiveable sin'. He is prone to think of himself as unworthy and a failure, and his developing sexuality can add fuel to the fire of this sense of failure.

When your son has a wet dream he may not have any sexual fantasy with it, but he may nevertheless wake up thinking of girls. This is part of his development as a mature sexual being. However, your son may interpret this as 'lust'. He may have been taught that it is wrong for him as a Christian to 'lust after a woman'. He may, in a confused way that he cannot express verbally, feel that his wet dream is all to do with his 'lust' and that he must be very sinful. Because teenagers are so vulnerable to feelings of sin and failure your son needs handling gently at a time like this. He is reacting as an unsure teenager and not as an adult, and you must treat him as such.

Encourage your teenager not to feed his fantasies. He does not need to go to sex shops nor does he need to read pornographic magazines to develop into a mature adult. This sort of stuff will rather promote retarded sexual development. Help him to understand that he is not being masculine by indulging himself in such material. Help him to see that this sort of material reduces man to less than God intended and planned because it takes something beautiful and exploits it to feed and fan sexual desires wrongly. If you are unable to talk to him yourself (which is likely, and he may prefer not to talk to parents) then try and ensure that someone else has sounded him out gently. This is a subject that may be covered in his youth group at church, at school, or when he is away at a church camp. However, it is a subject that may have been avoided if you come from a segment of Christian society in which these subjects are taboo. Do not allow your child to suffer from the taboo of pietistic silence — teach him purity and holiness but not narrow piety! Make sure that someone has reassured him; and if nothing else books are an alternative.

Masturbation

Another area in which your son is likely to feel guilty, and to develop a habit of guilt that will plague him all his life, is in the area of masturbation. It is reckoned that virtually all normal males have masturbated at some time or other in their lives. Most teenage boys experiment sexually through masturbation. Many adult Christian men masturbate, without feelings of guilt associated with the act.

Your son should not be allowed to feel that masturbation is an unforgiveable sin. It is probable that your attitude to this will be passed on to him, so it is vital that you sort out what you feel. It is important for you to try to think this through intellectually and biblically rather than emotionally, with any inherited prejudice colouring your thoughts.

The Bible says very little about masturbation. The few times it is mentioned are interpreted differently by different scholars. Christian teaching and opinion about masturbation varies enormously and is often coloured by personal feelings of guilt.

Some Christian leaders claim that masturbation is wrong. They believe that it is a selfish act, giving pleasure to oneself alone and to no one else. They would say that sexual intercourse is a shared act of love. For that reason they prefer not to masturbate (if they can avoid it) and to confine the satisfaction of their sexual desire to sexual intercourse within marriage.

Another group of mature Christian men regard masturbation as a habit they developed as teenagers, which they wish they had never started. They are plagued both by a sense of failure that this thing seems to have the upper hand and they are unable to lick it completely (when they are tired or under stress they 'fall' again). They are unhappy that as Christians this should apparently have dominion over them. With a feeling of frustration about this goes a feeling of guilt. There is the tendency to react, 'I've gone and let God down again. I've done it again . . . I've sinned again. . .' In some Christian men a vicious circle of 'failure' and then guilt occurs, which traps them much of their lives.

This is one area in which you can help your sons. If you are among those who feel that masturbation is 'wrong' (or that it is 'not right' for you) and you wish that you had never started the habit, then try to warn your sons about it. It is possible that they may be able to learn from you, and from your experience not to let themselves get into this habit.

This whole area is a difficult one. You, as a parent, will be coloured by your own beliefs. If you heavy-handedly condemn masturbation then your sons may feel guilty. They then may not dare to share with you the fact that this is something with which they have been experimenting. You, by blowing it all out of proportion, may make it appear bigger than it really is. It then assumes the proportions of enormous guilt to your vulnerable teenager. He may almost be looking for something on which to fasten his teenage sense of failure — and this gives him a good focal point. He will then not dare to share with you or anyone else. All you may have achieved is landing him with a load of guilt that God never intended him to have.

If you can enable your sons to see that this is one area they will appreciate having control over as adults, and therefore it is an area in which it is best not to form a habit, then you will have helped rather than hindered.

If you are among the rare breed of men who see masturbation as a positive and good gift from God — used rightly — then share this with your sons. You will be able to impart something enriching to your teenagers that they are unlikely to hear from others. Remember that if you are of this breed that you are treading on delicate ground. Make sure that the liberty that God has given to you is not taken and used to cause others to stumble. Help your teenager to understand that your views are not generally held, and that he would be unwise to spread them in the church youth group — by doing this others would be very confused, and probably not helped.

If your sons want to discuss the fantasies that sometimes accompany masturbation and wet dreams then be ready to talk to them. However, this is an area that they will rarely want to discuss with parents, and so be careful not to corner your son and force things out of him that he would prefer to keep secret from you. Such secrecy is normal and right about matters that are private and personal.

Fantasies

Your own attitudes to sexual fantasy will colour what you say to your children. Presumably, as a Christian you will not be feeding your sexual fantasy life in a way that you know God dislikes. Presumably, you refuse to look at pornographic material both because it is putting impure thoughts into your mind, and also because it is reducing women to sex objects instead of people. Presumably, you will be wary of erotic and of pornographic material because it arouses you sexually, and you as a Christian only want to find sexual satisfaction with your marriage partner. You will refuse to look at material depicting sadistic or masochistic sexual acts because you know that this is not what God intended or planned for man. Similarly, you will consider it undesirable to indulge your fantasy life in any sexual material that relates to deriving sexual satisfaction from someone of your own sex.

Ideally, your sexual fantasy life will centre around your partner in marriage. Other people will be seen as beautiful, and even as desirable, but will come into the category of unattainable because 'I am already committed for life'. Therefore, your fantasy life will not focus on others. It is quite normal not to have a sexual fantasy life. Some men and women do, and others do not.

If you are able to talk to your teenagers about this then you will be wanting to impart or at least imply certain standards to them.

Homosexual leanings

Try to help them to understand that at some stage in adolescence it is normal for teenagers to have a sexual orientation that is biased towards their own sex. A boy is not a homosexual because he has homosexual leanings during part of his teen years, most boys do. The same applies to girls. Help your children to understand the difference between homosexual orientation and homosexual practice. I believe that the Bible teaches that the adult with homosexual orientation is called to exercise restraint as much as the married adult Christian is called to sexual fidelity. The teenager who is passing through a phase of being attracted to someone of his own sex does not have to experiment with someone of his own sex. You may need to warn your sons to avoid situations in changing rooms, in which mutual masturbation is practised. This can then lead on to situations which your sons would prefer to avoid.

Unfortunately your boys are not growing up in an ideal world. You cannot insulate them from fallen humanity, and from the resulting impaired human relationships. If your son has a particularly attractive build (and there is a definite type) then he may need warning that adult men may find him attractive, so that he can extricate himself from situations when he might be alone with certain men. Try not to frighten him, but do try to make sure that either he knows how to look after himself or that he is not left alone in situations where he could be harmed. Places to watch are swimming baths, and the sea-side.

Guilt and sexuality

Help your teenager to have a positive affirmatory attitude towards his developing sexuality. If you have inherited hang-ups about your sexuality, then try not to pass them on to your children — they will go through life freer and more as God intended if you can manage to avoid passing your inhibitions on to them.

Help your children to see that guilt has a right place in their lives. A feeling of guilt is often the Holy Spirit telling Christians when they are doing wrong. However, don't allow guilt to be used as a blanket that stifles the Holy Spirit. Wrong guilt can so consume teenagers that they are unable to hear God's real voice because of the clamour of emotions exercised about the wrong things. It is probable that before you can help your teenagers that you will first have to sort yourself out. It will be worthwhile not only for them but also for you, and you will benefit immeasurably.

Unnecessary guilt

God does not intend anyone to go through life carrying an unnecessary load of guilt. Where there is real guilt about wrong which has been committed, then he intends us to accept the forgiveness he offers when we are really sorry and ask his forgiveness.

However, it is all too easy for Christian parents to impart guilt to their children without realising that this is happening. You may present your teenagers with standards that they cannot attain, and being vulnerable, they feel guilty for not being what you expect of them. You can make your children feel guilty about their apparent failure to live perfect Christian lives — especially if you allow them to assume that you, their parents, are perfect! I am convinced that God does not intend a teenager facing major exams to feel guilty for not spending an hour daily in prayer and Bible study. And yet some Christian teenagers feel guilt for this reason. Why does this sort of situation arise?

I believe that sometimes this particular feeling labelled 'guilt', is not the Holy Spirit speaking through someone's conscience. It is rather, a vulnerable teenager sensing failure about everything in general, and about his spiritual life in particular. When you let him know that you expect him as a Christian to conform to certain religious standards then it is likely that he will feel guilty for not living up to what he cannot do. If your children are brought up with the assumption, 'If I don't have a daily "quiet time" then my day will fail, and I will fail' then it is likely that at some time or other they will feel guilty. There will inevitably be days when they cannot spend time alone with God. You can help your child greatly in this respect. Help him to understand that Christianity is primarily about relationships, and especially that it is about one supreme relationship — that of an individual person with God. Your child must learn to relate to God as he walks to school, as he does the washing-up, as he mows the lawn, and as he faces life's joys and problems. He must learn how to bring God into every situation he encounters. Then he will find that it is ridiculous to feel guilty any day when he fails to have a daily 'God slot' in his life, when he is under particular pressure at school or at home. He must learn the value of having a regular time alone with God and with the Bible, but he must not be allowed to form the habit of feeling guilty if he has been unable to make this time.

It is easy for you with your enthusiasm and desire to help your child grow and mature as a Christian inadvertently to teach him to feel guilty — and this of course, is not what you intend him to feel. Help him positively and joyfully to find ways of deepening his personal knowledge of God, without feeling guilty for anything he has omitted to do. God delights in your child's knowledge of him, and I believe he does not want you to let your child feel guilty when he is not immediately perfect.

11: Your teenager's future

His mouth was firmly set: 'I'm going to see to it that my Paul gets all the chances in life that I never had . . . ', without a glance in the direction of his son, sitting in the corner.

Paul knew that his father meant well, but his sagging shoulders told their own story. He knew as well as I did that his father had no intention of letting him have a say in his own future. Long ago Paul had resigned himself to a situation which he was powerless to change. He knew that he could never be what his father hoped and planned for him. He knew that it was useless even attempting to help his father understand this. His father would listen but not take in what he heard. All Paul could do was to stay silent, and hope that his dad would leave him alone — knowing that he could never attain what was expected of him.

Paul's father represents one extreme of what many parents do to a lesser degree. Many try to turn their children into the adults that they themselves have failed to be.

Your motives
Paul's dad left school early because his own father was ill, and Paul's dad was needed to help support his family. University had been an impossible dream to him — a dream that he wanted to make real through his son. His plans for Paul sprang from two motives. He genuinely wanted the best for Paul and, as he saw it, that meant university education. He did not want Paul to miss some-

thing he had been unable to have purely for financial reasons.

Yet, to some degree, he was regarding Paul as an extension of himself. He wanted to live out the university life that he had missed through his son. Sadly, he failed to realise that this was what he was doing, or he would have relieved Paul of a heavy burden. Failing to consult Paul about what he really wanted to do with his life, his father would have been staggered to learn that Paul's one desire in life was to be a landscape gardener. And he would have been amazed that Paul only agreed to aim for university so as not to hurt him.

Since childhood it had been assumed that he would stay on at school and aim for 'O' and 'A' levels. No one had ever discussed any alternatives with him, and he felt disloyal at the thought of suggesting something different to his parents, who had gone without so much, so that he could enjoy all the benefits he now had.

What price academic success?

Parents have many different motives for wanting their children to succeed academically. At the highest and best it is so that their child will have the qualifications necessary for him to use his life as he wants to. This may, or may not, mean achieving academic success. At an even higher level it is so that the children of Christian parents will have the resources and qualifications they need to use their lives as God directs and leads. But God often guides teenages through the gifts, abilities and qualifications that he has already given to them.

You may need to think through your attitudes towards your children's education. Are you educating them so that they can live life to its full potential, or are you educating them for other reasons and towards other aims. Make sure that the element of 'keeping up with the Jones's does not enter into your planning for your childrens' schooling. It is possible even within church fellowship for parents to almost compete with one another over their children's education. It starts with getting them places at the 'best' schools, and progresses to getting them into university. This is especially so in churches which have a high percentage of members who are professional men and women. It may entail considerable loss of face and embarrass a lawyer if he has to confess: 'My son's going into the building trade — he wants to . . .' when the rest of the men's fellowship seem to be arguing about the relative merits of Durham versus Oxbridge universities. Never make your child feel he ought to go to university just so that you will feel accepted and at one with your church members or colleagues at work.

Beware of exerting subtle pressure on your children to conform to a certain type that makes it easy for you in turn to conform to the type who attend your church. If you are the only deacon whose daughter works in a supermarket (because she chooses not to use her gifts at university) then why should you feel ashamed? She is living her own life and not yours! The struggle to conform and be what you assume is expected of you may start early on. You may project it onto your children when they are young. If your area is one that has maintained the eleven plus exam you may feel that everyone's child has passed the eleven plus, and therefore you go through agonies in case you are the only parents in your circle whose child does not pass. If he fails — so what! He may grow up to be a far better member of adult society than those gaining multiple degrees. He may be the kind of person whose character exhibits the true kind of love about which the Apostle Paul writes in the Bible: love that is self-giving, and love that will contribute to healing in a society that is torn and hurting.

Never assume that the best pathway for your child to follow is necessarily that of academic success. It is possible that this is the best way for him, but be ready for the possibility that it is not.

Parental pressure

While your child is still at school your job is to quietly encourage him. Try to establish a balance between encouraging him to exert himself so that he will achieve the best he can, and fussing and pushing him to try and gain higher marks than his ability warrants. Your child has enough pressure at school without coming home to face that of over-anxious parents who try to force him to be better than he can ever hope to be.

Support your child in his school work, and help him to make the best use of the time, talents and resources available to him. Never let your child feel that he has either let you, or his teacher, down if he does not do as well as is expected of him. Do not let him feel a failure if his exam results are poor.

Your child may be very sensitive to the standards that have been set by older or younger brothers and sisters. He may constantly feel that he is being compared with them. He may feel pleased when he does better than them, but a total failure if he cannot meet their standards. Never let him feel inferior to them.

God sees your child as an individual. God does not compare your child with his siblings. Try to be like this yourself!

Your child's character

At this point, praying for your child's future can seem confusing. You may pray anxiously and impatiently, 'Dear God, please let him pass those exams. . .' It seems such a right and proper prayer. But it is just possible that God wants to do things with your child's life that he can only do if he fails those exams — which seem all-important at the time. Try not to dictate to God what his future for your child ought to be. Be flexible enough to realise that God's plans may well be different from yours.

It will be hard for you to be willing for your child to use his life exactly as God has told him to if this involves him in doing something that your family has never done

109

before. It may be as hard for you to accept him being a career missionary overseas as it is for you to accept that he is going to work in a demolition firm. God needs Christian demolition experts as well as career missionaries and university graduates.

If your teenager announces firmly that he is going to leave school at sixteen it will not be easy for you to accept it, if your family traditionally has worked for academic achievement. Be ready to talk this through in depth both with him and with his school, and try to understand the reasons lying behind his desire. He may, or may not, have valid reasons. Give him the benefit of the doubt, if you are unsure. God usually guides through common sense, and children tend to follow the accepted pattern within their family structure. However, be ready and flexible enough to let your child be the exception to your family's rule, if it really seems the right thing for him to do. Be ready to back your child and support him when grandparents cannot understand what has 'gone wrong' (as they will see it). Don't make him feel he is the family drop-out.

Ignorance does not help parents in professions. Apprenticeships, and training on the job, are concepts that may be rejected by such parents because they are foreign — not because they have been assessed as useless. It is possible that your child will do better in life, and as a human being, if he started a job on leaving school, and then attended a course at the local polytechnic, on a day release basis. Do not reject this because you knew nothing of such schemes when you were young.

Surely it is more important that your teenager should turn out to be happy and a good influence in society than that he should clutter up the end of his name with impressive lists of degrees, and yet have no idea of how real people live and interact.

Of course exams are important but be careful not to put so much pressure on your child to do well in exams that he assumes that exam pass or failure, is the be all and end all of his existence. As Christian parents you should be as concerned to see the fruit of the Spirit developing in your child's life, as you are about anything else. You should be longing, praying and helping the development of qualities like love, joy, peace, longsuffering, goodness, gentleness and faith. Help him to know that these are important to you. Do not push academic success so much that his values become distorted.

If your child can learn never to exploit other people in order to gain his own desires, if he can learn to put other people before himself, and to do a good day's work for a good day's pay, then he will be the kind of adult that this world needs. He may contribute more to society than anyone doing research about obscure subjects irrelevant to life, or those who trample people underfoot to gain success for themselves.

In his majesty's service
As you aim to help your child to become the kind of adult that God wants him to be, then you will need God's guidance yourself. God often guides teenagers through their parents' advice and so it is imperative that you yourselves seek to understand God's plan for your child's future, as well as encouraging him to do the same. Pray about it together as a family, so that all of you unitedly seek God's will (assuming that your teenager wants God mentioned at this stage of his life).

You may feel that because you dedicated your child to God when he was a baby that this is all there is to it. You may find that now he is a young adult, and making decisions about his career, that once again you, his parents, must privately re-dedicate him to God for God to use as he wants. Firstly, you may have to dedicate yourselves to God in order to relinquish what you personally want for your child. God cannot show you his plan until you are willing for this. You cannot say to God, 'Show me what you want and then I'll decide whether or not to back up my teenager in it. If I disapprove of your plans then of course you can't expect my support. . . '

111

Hearing God's call

If you sense that God may be calling your child into full-time Christian service then think and pray carefully about motivation. It is possible that long ago you once heard God calling you and that you rejected that calling. It is reasonable for you to help hope that your child will now do what you know you should have done. But do not encourage your child to do this to ease your sense of guilt or failure, make sure that he is following God's call and not parental pressure.

If you want to be Mr-super-Christian (and who doesn't) in your church, then what could apparently be better than having a son or daughter engaged in some glamorous Christian adventure, like working with refugees overseas or translating Bibles into unknown languages. Never encourage your child to do this kind of work because at the back of your mind you know it will enhance your standing as a Christian. It is just possible that your child is so anxious to please you that he might do something like this that is right in itself but wrong if done for wrong motives. Your child would head for disaster because this might not be God's plan for his life.

Some parents succeed in living lives that deceive even themselves. God tells them to do something, and they respond: 'God, here am I . . . send my child!' It is inconvenient in mid-career to give up a safe job and venture out on one of the mad adventures God sometimes asks his followers to embark on for him. The easiest way out is for you to say: 'Well God, there's the mortgage you know . . . and I'm responsible to make sure my pension will be adequate so I must earn as much as I can until I retire . . . you understand that, don't you God. It would be a much better idea if I got my son to go instead of me. . . ' But, it was you, with your experience, that God called. Had you obeyed God then he would have seen to it that you would have survived with what seems, at present, to be an inadequate pension. Your child cannot do the job for which God has carefully equipped and trained you all your life. God may call your child to work alongside you but that is a bonus that you cannot expect until you have taken the costly step of obeying.

People before paper
To God, character is far more important than exam grades. As Christian parents, help your children to understand that you too feel this way. Try to adopt this as a basic attitude within your entire family. Let no one ever be judged in terms of worth by exam grades or the degrees they have achieved.

Help your teenagers to see that God does use brilliant men and women in his service. But also help them to understand that it is often those who have faced the most failure who are the people God has used in the past to achieve strategic major advances for him. As you do this, you will not only be helping your children themselves, but you will also be teaching them an attitude that is important for life — that people themselves matter more than their achievements.

12: Support through school

Jekyll and Hyde

It is a sad fact of life that many children have to start at new schools at a time when it would be best for them as people to stay in their old schools with trusted friends and familiar teachers. The age at which children move up to secondary schools is an age when many of them have problems enough in adjusting to the changes that their hormones are bringing about in their bodies, without having to learn to cope in new school situations.

When your child changes schools between eleven and thirteen years old then he may settle in quite happily, or he may be dogged by months of unhappiness and inability to cope with new surroundings and new people.

If your child has not settled into his new school then this may be reflected in his producing a lower standard of school work than is usual for him. If you find that his marks are lower than you think they should be then refrain from saying so! Try not to nag him about this, and be as patient as possible. Make sure that at home his life is free from strain and tension. Above all this means trying to ensure that you, as a married couple, are free from conflict with each other (if there is tension between the two of you then your teenager will sense it, and it will add to his general misery.)

You may feel that staff at the new school are to blame for your child's failure to do as well as you think he should. This may, or may not, be the case. Whatever happens do not criticise the staff in front of him, at this point. Try and increase his confidence in the new teachers at his new school, and help him to develop a positive attitude towards them.

If you feel that you have real grounds for complaint, or that there is something wrong with the way your teenager is being taught, then go to the staff concerned yourself. It is often best to make the initial approaches through the headmaster. You may feel that your child is being discriminated against, or being treated unfairly. Remember that you do not go to school to do battle for your child's rights. You rather go to try to help the staff teach your child most effectively. Be prepared for the fact that a staff member may put the blame on your child! There is the point of view of the member of staff (who may be right) as well as the point of view of your child, and the two may conflict.

Be careful how you talk to your child about this. He may be very embarassed if he finds out that you have talked to the school authorities about him, and it may be unnecessary for you to tell him. Never let your child gain the impression that the reason he is doing badly at work is because he is being taught inadequately . . . or if you have to tell him this out of honesty, then handle it wisely. You do not want him to learn the lesson from this incident that whenever he does badly at anything it is someone else's fault — hardly a lesson to help prepare him to accept responsibility for his actions as an adult.

Try never to set yourself *against* your child's school. Always try to work with the staff, for your child's good, and aim to support both the staff and your child. It is important to help mould your child's thinking about why he is trying to do well at school, and this will shape his future attitudes towards work.

Children usually respond to incentives, which can be pleasant or unpleasant. He may do well in class to try to please you, or to please a certain teacher whom he respects and whose praise he values. Alternatively he may work hard and do well because he is afraid of the shame of doing badly, or of possible punishment.

Deprivation can be a form of punishment. 'If you pass

that exam with good marks then I'll buy you a cassette radio' can be interpreted as 'If you fail then you will be deprived of the chance of a cassette radio'.

Never let your child fear that he will be deprived of your love if he does not attain a given standard in school work — parental love must not be dependent on exam marks, or a child will develop warped values as an adult.

Make sure that your teenager knows you love him whether he does well or not in school work. Also, make sure that your love does not depend on his achieving at games or club activities. Parental love must be love that has no strings attached.

In a theological sense you, the father of your child, represent God to him. Your child's concepts of God the Father will be coloured by the quality of your fathering. Your child depends on you for all that he needs physically and emotionally, as an adult Christian learns in another sense to depend on God the Father. God's love is unconditional: He loves us as we are with no strings attached. The child who feels 'Daddy will only love me when I'm a good boy' has enormous problems as an adult in accepting the fact that God loves him whether he is 'good' or not.

In another sense a child's obedience to his father is obedience and respect for God the Father, about whom he is learning. In childhood he honours God by his attitude towards his human father (although he is unaware of this). As an adult he decides whether to give the same respect and obedience to God or not — and whether to follow God himself or not.

Your child probably wants to please you, his father. This is an attitude he can carry over into his adult life, when he may decide to follow God, and then wants to act in a manner which pleases his Heavenly Father. The child who has learned the joy of pleasing dad, finds it joyful and liberating to try and live in a manner which pleases his Heavenly father in adult life.

If your child works hard at school to please you, then encourage him in this. He is developing an attitude which, later on, will help him to want to work in a way that pleases God. His motive will not be fear of punishment, or shame if others do better than he does, but rather the simple desire that what he does (and the way in which he does it) will please his Father God. This vital ingredient is one you can instil into your children's attitudes when they are young, and it will benefit them in adult life.

This is the ingredient that turns a routine boring job into one that is satisfying. It helps the worker to know that the way in which he is doing his job is in a manner that pleases God, brings honour to Him, and is therefore (no matter how dull) potentially valuable.

Few parents sit down and analyse the attitudes they are unconsciously imparting to their children — but maybe you need to do just that! The little things that you gloss over as you say them may be the very words that mark your children for life.

Disrupting difficulties

School reports about your teenager may baffle you: 'Sounds like a different child — could they have muddled up the reports?' you may ask each other.

It is not uncommon for teenagers to be different at home and school. They are adept at Jekyll and Hyde acts. The teenager who is unruly and defiant at school may be pliant and easy at home. The child who is a pain in the neck at home may be a model of good behaviour at school.

If your home is a place in which your child finds the atmosphere emotionally draining then he may be tense and difficult at home. School, with its impersonal atmosphere may be a welcome relief to him, and this may show in the difference in his behaviour in the two places.

If home is tense and difficult for your child then he may react by doing his school work very badly, or he may react in the opposite way and escape home tension by over-working and attaining high marks. Teenagers find tension at home hard to handle. Do your best to eliminate this, working at all the different relationships in your family — you cannot smooth them over with hypocrisy — or by pretending problems do not exist — you can genuinely help by working at sorting them out.

My husband and sons are marvellous at detecting the different undercurrents of tension within our family. Even if their efforts at sorting out problems are misguided at times, at least they try very hard — so hard that at times the two females among us do not ever want to hear one or other of them saying, 'Blessed are the peace-makers' again. We do, however, recognise and value their vital role as family peace-makers!

If you do not know whether or not your teenager is 'normal' for his age, then be assured that this is a perfectly normal reaction from the parents of teenagers! No two are alike, and you cannot expect your teenager to be like another one. Even within a family the children will differ vastly in their maturity and development in their teen years.

If you are genuinely worried about your teenager, and wonder if there may be something psychiatrically wrong with him, or whether he (or you) need 'child guidance' then you will be wise to go and talk to the teachers who know him at school. Again this is usually best done through the head of the school. The school staff have more experience of teenagers than you have, and they will be able to confirm or deny your fears on an objective unemotional basis.

Do remember that school problems will be reflected in behaviour at home, and home problems will be reflected at school. Of major trauma to your teenager is any lack of harmony between you as marriage partners. Any disruption of home life is damaging to an adolescent. Separation or divorce by parents will damage children of any age but some people claim that teenagers are more vulnerable to hurt than children of any other age (this cannot, and has not been proved but sounds plausible).

Responses to stress

Poor school work may result from many other things as well. Important matters like a quarrel with a best friend or the break up of a boy-girl relationship can result in disaster in exams. Excess anxiety over exams sometimes leads to good results due to the extra adrenaline flowing round the body, but it more often leads to bad results that do not reflect the child's true potential. If your teenager cannot get on with a member of staff then this may be reflected in a low exam mark.

During teenage years the development of your child's sexual emotions may lead to an upheaval of his whole personality. This may result in difficulty in studying, and in behaviour problems at school. Be as patient as you can as he goes through all this — he is not having a very happy time either (and neither are the staff teaching him probably).

You must understand your child's personality if you are going to help him through all of this. Different people react in different ways to the same situations, because of their different personality make-ups. You should know your child better than anyone else. Most teenagers, from time to time, go through stages when they feel overwhelmed by the stresses they face in life. Reactions to this vary. Some become depressed and may even make suicide attempts to end life (although the teenager at the time genuinely wishes to die). Other teenagers become aggressive, apathetic or resentful — and they make sure that you know how they feel!

Try to understand your teenager well enough to see the reasons why he is reacting as he is. As you understand his behaviour take it seriously, but do be prepared to see the funny side (away from him, of course). The funny side, that you ought to be able to laugh at is the side of yourself that your teenager may well be revealing. You may see in him yourself at your worst and angriest! And if you are able to laugh (not in front of him, and not to under-estimate his distress) then it will help you handle yourself. In your teenager you will often discover some of your less lovable traits.

Going to meetings

Make sure that you take every opportunity to build good relationships with the staff at your child's school. Attend all the meetings that are arranged for you to discuss your child with the staff that teach him. Try not to give priority to church meetings over your child's meetings at his school for you and his staff. (I did say 'church' and not 'God'. God must be given priority in your life as a Christian parent — but many Christian parents equate church meetings with God, and believe that by not putting a meeting first they are not putting God first!)

It is important for your child to know that you are interested enough in his life and progress at school to give it priority over church meetings, and even some work commitments. The Christian parent who is in a position of Christian leadership is leading a lot of other parents, and they are likely to follow his lead in assessing the priority that should be given to parent-school relationships.

Keep a close liaison with your child's school but do not be so stiflingly close that your child feels he has no independent existance apart from you — even at his school.

Make sure that you go to speech days, parents' open days, school plays and to fund raising events. Your child needs to know that you care enough for him to do this. If you do attend he will probably say little. If you do not go then you will find he is badly hurt that you could not be bothered to attend when 'all the other parents went'.

Your child will be especially vulnerable to your non-appearance at school events if you attend church functions regularly. It is good, right and proper for you to attend these — but never let your child feel that you have time and energy for these but none for him. This hardly encourages a positive attitude towards God and church.

If you do not understand something that is going on at school then ask rather than criticise or worry. If you receive a school report with the words no normal average parent can cope with, 'He could do better', then go and ask what it means in this situation and with this child! There are many reasons for these words being written — so find out before jumping to the wrong conclusions.

Responsible actions

You may feel that you ought to be even more closely involved with your child's education. Start off by supporting the Parent Teacher Association and, if you feel that God wants you to, be willing to be on one of its committees. Remember though, firstly, that your teenager might prefer you not to be so closely involved with his school. If appropriate ask his opinion (and even permission) before offering yourself in this way. Secondly, you may find that close involvement with the PTA clashes with church activities. Make sure that you do not take on more than you can reasonably handle. Weigh in the balance the fact that unless there is Christian representation on the PTA, there may be no Christian voice to be heard through that PTA — and possibly God wants your mouth to provide that voice.

Parent governors now sit on some school governing bodies. In a few schools Christian parents have accepted the post of parent governor. Perhaps God wants you to do this. I am sure that he wants you to seek his guidance about whether or not you should do this, even if his answer is an eventual 'no'. Unless Christians are involved in educational policy making Christian ethical standards will not necessarily be adopted in the pluralistic society of today.

Working with a school to help your child attain his full potential is fulfilling and worthwhile. At least it is in the end, once your child has passed adolescent storms!

13: Coping with exams

Many teenagers live life in glorious technicolour, or at times in intense black while their parents and other adults plod along untroubled in a grey fog. Your life may seem intensely dull to your teenager while his may seem such a whirl of activity to you that you are left gasping at the sight of all he does — even though no one expects you to keep up with him.

Sorting out priorities

If he is caught up in excessive activity he may need help in sorting out priorities, and the best use of his time. If he is still at school and working for CSE, 'O' or 'A' levels then he will need your support in helping him to get over the mountain of study that is required. He is unlikely to welcome your interference in his social life, or any unasked advice you throw at him on how he should spend out of school hours. However, he may require tactful help from someone. Unfortunately this is one area in which he probably cannot afford the luxury of learning by making mistakes. A job, or a place at polytechnic or university may depend on exam results; and none of these can be lost lightly since the opportunity may not be repeated.

If you are able and if your child responds positively to you, then try to talk to him gently about the amount of work he is (or is not) doing. Avoid speaking so vehemently that he immediately does the opposite of what you suggest; you are treading on delicate ground. Possibly it is best for someone at school (his teacher or Head) to talk to him about homework. He may respond positively, knuckle under, and work to pass important exams.

The value of school trips
School life also puts demands on parents. You are likely to find that your teenager comes home from school with monotonous regularity, stating, airily, 'Dad, I need £75. . . ' . While you try and look impassive, wondering what ever he has broken, he continues, 'Everyone's going on a field trip'. A trip to France, skiing holiday, down the mines, bird-watching, hunting the Lochness monster . . . you name it and he'll say everyone is going to do it!

If you are wise you will work out your approach to such demands ahead of time. No one can wisely steward the money given to a family by God, and then blow it on endless 'school trips'. No matter what your teenager says to the contrary you must assess whether or not each proposed trip is necessary for the exams for which he is studying. If the trip is necessary then it is possible that your local education authority will refund part (or all) of the cost involved, after the trip has been made. If it is part of his syllabus then you must try and let him go, as school work for the rest of the year may be based on the research he worked on, and material gathered on that trip. If you face genuine financial problems then talk to the member of staff involved, or to the Head: money may be available from a special source for your child.

Other school trips that do not form part of learning for an exam can be a marvellous educative experience for your child. However you need to assess them in a different light. Some families regard such school trips in the category of 'holiday'. Therefore, those families deduct the cost of a school trip from the amount of money that is being saved in family budgeting for annual holidays. Your teenager must then decide whether or not to choose a school skiing holiday instead of your family holiday. This helps him to understand that money for school activities does not grow on trees (any more than money for food does) and that it is all part of family budgeting. When he claims: 'Everyone is going sailing . . . ' you can safely interpret this as meaning: 'Most parents are panicking like us — a few have the cash and their children can go — but the majority are like us. . .' Help your teenager to understand that he is under no obligation to do the same as 'everyone'.

School trips are especially valuable to your child, so encourage them if possible. They give him the chance to get right away and to stay away from home and family, perhaps for the first time. He is supervised (as much as the staff can manage, which varies from school to school), but at least he will not try out some of the more stupid things he might try if he was on his own alone for the first time in his life. The price you pay is that of not having your teenager with you for your annual holiday — something you probably regret but which may delight him. Teenagers rarely rate a family holiday at the top of the charts for their summer activities. It is expected of them and so they go to oblige: and usually manage to enjoy it despite expressed or silent misgivings.

There is a wide variety of 'Christian' camps, house-parties, and holidays of different kinds, which your teen-ager might enjoy more than a family summer holiday. Be ready to free him to go if he would like to. Again he will learn much that he can only learn away from home and away from you.

Preparing for exams

In encouraging your child to make the best use of his time, talents, and family resources you will have to help him when it is time for him to study for exams. This will involve a degree of sacrifice and consideration on your part. To study he will need somewhere away from the bustle of family life where he can settle down with his books, and work in the way that most suits him. Some teenagers appear able to study in front of a tele-vision set in the living room — but the majority cannot.

Make sure that your teenager has a warm and peaceful place where he can work at night. You may have to go without the tv yourselves if the living room is the only warm place. Try to work out, as a family, how much tv viewing should go on week nights, and then plan a daily programme of who will watch what, and when. This saves the set being on non-stop, and your teenager failing to get round to studying. Encourage him to work out a timetable for study and to assess how much he will aim to do and how long it will take. Get him to set himself both short and long-term goals to aim for. Do not plan your teenager's revision programme for him. Encourage and support him as he works but never play detective to see if he has done what he ought to have done during his homework. He must learn how to study on his own, and how to plan this himself. If he does not learn before he leaves school then he will have a difficult time for the rest of his life.

In contrast to you, your teenager can perhaps work better with his radio or cassette player blaring full blast. He is not really listening to the words or the music, but the noise supports him as he studies. Even the chat of disc-jockeys does not really interrupt his study; if he feels lonely and isolated with his books then the disc-jockey's presence in his room can provide a form of friendship that is encouraging at this time.

As exams draw nearer you will probably need unobtrusively to re-organise the running of your home to fit even more round your teenager's specific needs. Try to keep things running smoothly, and request his help at home as little as possible during these vital weeks — unless he needs the break and relaxation of doing the washing-up. Make sure that before, and during, exams you do not fill the house with visitors — even a visit from a loved granny and grandpa may be a slight disruption and that little can be enough to interfere with his need of peace and quiet. Keep your personal involvement with church activities under strict control at these times. Do not arrange to be away, or out every night on church business, before or during exams. Your teenager needs the support of both parents at this critical time.

However, don't let him know that you are re-organising your lives for a few weeks to make his as easy as possible.

'Exam nerves'

The nearer he comes to major exams, the more nervous your teenager is likely to be. There is one sense in which a degree of nervousness is good since each person has an optimum level of tension which enables him to perform at his best. Less than this means that he is not doing as well as he might. This is one reason why it is unwise to tranquillise your teenager with any pills you may have around the house. It is unwise for many other reasons as well to have pills of any kind accessible to young people.

If your daughter suffers from pre-menstrual tension then it is possible that this will affect her exam performance, if crucial exams occur during days of PMT. If this is a problem for your daughter then get her to see her doctor months before the exams. Simple treatment like extra vitamin B, or diuretic medicine may help greatly. If your doctor is treating your daughter for severe PMT then he may feel it necessary to write a letter for the examination board explaining the situation. This may, or may not, make a difference, but there is no harm in informing an examination board of genuine cases of severe pre-menstrual tension. Five per cent of teenagers are very badly affected by 'exam nerves'. If your child is one of these, then take him to your doctor sooner rather than later. Modern medicines can help your child without affecting his capacity for study or for writing exam papers.

The reasons why some teenagers are unable to cope with exams are many. Some are unable to cope with all that has been demanded of them, and have been taught more material than they can absorb. Even the amount that they have managed to learn may be swamped by a mass of further information that has been stuffed into them. They may panic when this happens.

Some teenagers are, in one simple word — lazy. This

may not have dawned on them until they suddenly realise that they have been deluding themselves into thinking that they have been studying enough, when in fact they have not. They suddenly become acutely aware of pages of unlearned facts and figures; and flounder in the maze of information that they cannot possibly memorise in time for the exams. No wonder panic sets in. If your child comes into the 'lazy' category, then do not lose heart. He may fail the exam for which he is sitting, but this failure may be exactly what he requires as an incentive to shock him into life and its realities. He may, for the first time, face the fact that he cannot drift through life without really working to achieve his aim. This is a hard but necessary lesson for some.

Other children panic about exams because well-meaning parents have wrapped them in cotton wool all their lives and over-protected them. If you have come to the rescue regularly and done his homework for him if he cannot do it, if you have kept him home almost every time he has a cold or a headache, and so on, then facing a major unknown like an exam may be an overwhelming experience for him.

Other children fear exams because, for years, the whole of school and home life have been geared towards exam success. You, his parents, may have talked incessantly about exams, and he dreads failing and letting you down. If his brothers and sisters have done well then he may dread doing less well than them, and fear rejection by the family if he fails.

Parents' provision
Try to ensure that around exam times that home does not become an extension of school. Help your teenager to feel extra secure and loved at this time but don't go to extremes and smother him. Be ready to listen if he wants to talk about problems with revision. Provide him with the little things that will make his life easier at this time — things like comfort, warmth, favourite foods, and a milky night drink to help him sleep.

Some teenagers sleep badly around exam times. Try providing him with a special time in which he can relax before sleep and after the evening's study. A walk round the block with father, or a chat in the kitchen with mum may provide all that is needed. A hot bath, or an hour in front of the tv, may help his racing mind to slow down and his body to relax ready for sleep. If he faces major problems with sleep then encourage him to see a doctor. Do not give him any sleeping pills you may have as they may be unsuitable for him.

During the exams themselves be as thoughtful and tolerant as possible. Keep household tension as minimal as possible. Arrange your life so that you can act as chauffeur if necessary to avoid a long walk, a bike, bus or train journey. Free him from household duties if necessary. Provide him with anything he is allowed to take in to eat during the exam. Make sure that important small things are remembered. Has he a sweater in case it is cold, and has he a thin shirt on in case a heatwave hits? Has he wound his watch, so that it does not stop in the middle of the exam — disrupting his carefully planned timetable. Try not to fuss, but do ensure your child has all he needs.

Make sure that your teenager knows you are praying for him during his exams. No matter what his religious beliefs are at this stage, he will be grateful for this support. Note exact exam times and let him know that you intend to try to pray for him specifically during the papers themselves. If he is a committed Christian then creatively bring God into his exam time. Pray with him about exams. He will appreciate ideas like giving him a little card on each exam day with a Bible verse on it. He will be helped by the knowledge that God will help him through the exam period, and that providing he has worked hard, the results will form part of God's guidance about his whole future.

If your child is an enthusiastic Christian in his teens then you may have a tricky situation to handle. Of course you want him to be 100 percent committed to God, and living life fully for him. But you still want your child to find time for down-to-earth activities like doing the washing-up, and working at his homework. It is important that he learns that Christianity is supremely about developing a growing relationship with Jesus Christ, rather than attending an excessive number of prayer meetings and Bible studies. Help him to understand that the purpose of his Christian life is to bring glory to God, and that God is not glorified if homework is sloppy and rushed so that he can attend church meetings. Talking to your teenager about balance in anything is hard. Little is harder than seemingly to dampen his vibrant enthusiasm for Jesus Christ (the kind of enthusiasm you once experienced and wish could return again).

You have a vital role to play in helping your child through his years at school, and as he faces exams at the end of his school life. There is much that remains your responsibility that you can never hand over to teachers. Your child is your child and he always needs you.

14: Leaving school

When your teenager leaves school he may face an interminable wait for exam results, which will determine his immediate future, or he may join Britain's jobless young people, or hopefully he may walk straight into work.

A final fling of youth

Weeks of waiting for exam results, after a teenager has left school, are weeks of tension for the teenager himself and (be honest with yourselves) they are also weeks of tension for you, his parents. Make major allowances for each member of the family, and for the fact that you all face stress while you wait. So much hangs on the results that it is almost impossible not to be tense about them. Try to root yourself in the assurance that God has a plan for your teenager's future. If he is able to enter into this assurance with you, then encourage him to do so. If however, he is hostile to your Christian faith then express your confidence in God but do so in a low key.

The holiday after your teenager leaves school can be a special time for him, especially if he does not start work immediately. Encourage him to do something more adventurous than is usual during this time. Restrain the little voice inside you that claims: 'This is probably our last family summer holiday together, so let's make sure that we all get together and do something as a family'. Clinging onto your teenager's past childhood in the wrong way may produce the opposite of what you desire. Be willing to let your teenager free to have a holiday on his own if he wants to. Encourage him to think adventurously at this phase of life. It is probably his last opportunity for a real adventure, before adult life lays its claims and responsibilities on him. Do not dampen his enthusiasm if he has (what seems to you) wild plans to cycle from Land's End to John O'Groats, or to work for the summer as a volunteer in an old people's home, or to offer his services to a missionary society for the summer, or to go and harvest grapes in Italy. This is probably the only time when he will be able to express his sense of adventure, and have the adult maturity to be able to carry a project through sensibly.

Once the exam results are out — after two months of holiday — he will no longer be free for a final fling of youth and adult concerns will tie him down.

Facing exam results

As the exam results draw relentlessly nearer try to keep your anxiety to yourself. Do not add a burden to your teenager's own worries by letting him feel that he has to carry your concern as well as his own. Be ready to give him strength at this time of waiting. If he seems his usual self then do not assume he is unconcerned. He may be acting well and masking his anxiety to try to keep you calm. Accept the fact that he may not know how to handle feelings of fear of failure and rejection if he fails. By now, he ought to know that your love for him is not dependent on exam results, but fear of rejection may lurk at the back of his mind all the same.

It is sensible to plan your summer holidays so that you are at home when the results come out. This does need planning a year ahead. Nothing ruins a potentially good holiday more than waiting every day for exam results to arrive, and it is even worse if the results bring failure. Do not be away yourself, leaving your teenager at home alone to face the results. No matter how independent of you he may seem, your unobtrusive presence can be a great moral support to him. Even if he snaps at you: 'Why don't you leave me alone. . .', remain unobtrusively present.

Decisions and procedure

Try to be organised about all the things that have to be done once exam results are out. If your teenager is planning to go to college then make sure you know what must be done if 'A' level grades attained are the ones needed, but even more important know what to do if they are not attained. Familiarise yourself with the process of 'UCCA clearing', and get to know the courses offered by local polytechnics and technical colleges. Know what must be done if 'UCCA clearing' does not produce a university place for your child. This will save you from unnecessary panic should this happen. It is a time when school staff are often away on their summer holiday and possibly not available to help parents. Check with the school though as some have a staff member available to advise after 'O' and 'A' level results are out. If your child has the 'A' level grades required by the college of his choice and a firm place is offered, then make sure that you know how to apply for a local education authority grant, and that you have the forms ready. If you have an accountant then he will help you with the forms which are means tested.

Be careful to be unobtrusive about the way you help your teenager at this time. He must make all the major decisions himself, and help received from you must be taken because he wants it, and not because you have taken the running of his life into your hands.

Assessing his qualities

When he is making important decisions about his future career, your teenager may have little information on which to base his decisions. Make sure he knows exactly what is involved in his choice of career (if he has the luxury of choice in a situation of high unemployment). Expose him to alternatives, if possible, and in an ideal world — where there are enough jobs to go round — try to let him defer his final choice of career until as late as possible. Meanwhile, until an ideal situation exists, help him to be grateful for any work he gets on a depressed job market.

Your teenager's sense of identity includes the formation of a self-image that projects into the future, and will lead him (unless prevented) down a certain pathway. Help him to develop his self-image realistically: especially to face the fact that he may not get a job for which he is aiming. Help him not to rely too much on a particular job for the fulfilment of his self-image. Make sure that he is not living in a dream world that will land him in inevitable failure and disappointment.

Help your teenager to assess himself and his good and bad qualities realistically. Then stand by him as he plucks up courage to try to attain what he is aiming at, and to run the risk of failing if he does not achieve his goal. If he plays safe and does not aim high, the risk is minimised. But he may then land a job in which he will be bored and frustrated for the rest of his life. Help him to make the most of his gifts and to attain the best possible. Help him to find the balance between attempting something that is unrealistic and too hard for him, and doing easy things that are not challenging and never help him to realise his full potential.

A first job

Your teenager may have left school, and not be planning to go on for further education. If he is starting his first job then he has tremendous adjustments to make. Be patient with him as he handles the emotional adjustments involved in coping with the change from a life of dependence at school to one of independence in the working world. Many teenagers find it hard to exert the self-discipline necessary to make the effort to prepare themselves for skilled work. Your teenager needs your support and encouragement through this rather than nagging and complaints when he fails.

Your teenager's first day at work is an important milestone both for him and for you. Nothing will ever be quite the same again. Not only must he make a new kind of relationship at home with the family, but he also has to learn how to handle new relationships with his friends and with people at work. At school he always knew that the staff were interested in him. Teachers always noticed him, even if it was only to complain that his writing was illegible, and his shoes needed cleaning. At work he will probably start off as the lowest of the low, and he is unlikely to enjoy this experience, or expect it to happen to him. He may feel that he is only a minute cog in a huge impersonal wheel, and that hardly anyone knows of his existence, let alone cares about him. His boss may seem a remote figure, he may find that discipline at work is more rigid than anticipated, and the illusion of being free at work proves to be a dream. Some teenagers feel disillusioned and humiliated by their first experience of work. They thought that at last they had entered the world of adults, where everything would be wonderful. Instead they face a hard slog, a daily grind. If your teenager is going through this, he may be difficult to live with. He may be bad-tempered, moody and irritable. Don't lecture him and make him feel even more of a failure than work has made him feel. Try to accept the fact that (paradoxically) he has complimented you by being at his nastiest at home: he can trust you enough to be at his worst with you. He feels safe enough with you to get his bad feelings out of his system. Be as tolerant and as understanding as you can. This phase will pass.

You may be able to help your teenager if you find out that he is facing problems with people at work. You have one thing he may value at this time that he normally spurns — your experience of life. He is inexperienced at handling people, and you may be able to help him to see where he is going wrong, if he can share these problems with you. The commonest reason why young people get the sack from work is because they cannot get on with other people. An adolescent tends to be intolerant and refuses to compromise. He needs to learn how to handle these two attitudes, since most adults need to be tolerant and to be willing to compromise to some degree in their working lives. At school and at home he may have been protected from the realities of the working world. Swearing, dirty stories and jokes, and the like may disturb him. Try to help him to be ready to enter a world that holds values which are different from those held at home. Try to help him to know how to handle this change. Piety will not help him. If he is a Christian then he must understand how to live out his faith positively but not judgementally. Help him to assess which things he is unaccustomed to doing for the reason that they are culturally unacceptable to you, and then to assess what things should not be done because he is a Christian. He will then be in a better position to know areas he should avoid, and which areas he can enter with work friends and colleagues.

You, and his home, are very important to him at this stage. Let him feel the security and the stability of home. Learn to accept him if he comes home with words and ideas that you do not like. If he comes home the worse for drink then handle the situation tactfully. Given time and love, your teenager will come through this transitional stage with no major problems.

Real money
You may have to be very patient with your teenager's apparent inability to handle money. His first wage packet may well be the first real money he has ever earned. He will probably have to learn by hard experience that once he has spent his money that there is none left! He also needs to understand the dangers of getting into debt.

Your teenager probably only learns by trial and error how to handle his money. Hopefully you have already prepared him for this. Don't get upset if it appears that all your teaching about budgeting has gone for nothing: he may be doing the opposite of what you have taught him just to see whether you were correct or not.

Once he is earning he should contribute realistically to the household expenses, if he is still living at home.

You are doing him no real favours by letting him live at home free, or cheaply. He must learn how to handle real money in an adult way. He must learn as quickly as possible how to budget for himself, how to live within his means, and how to make ends meet. If you do not want your teenager's money for yourself, then you could accept proper payment for home expenses, and quietly invest the money for him as a gift at a later date. This nest-egg could be a wonderful surprise later on.

Learning to save money is an important lesson middle-class parents often feel their teenagers should learn. Unfortunately our present level of inflation, with savings diminishing in their future buying power, will not encourage your teenager to save money.

Pressures from advertising

Your teenager is unlikely to emerge unscathed by the media's attempts to attract him as a consumer. His love of show and glamour are exploited, and little concern is shown for his real needs or his welfare. Advertising concentrates on the areas in which teenagers are most vulnerable. It is often directed at his immature sexual emotions, his insecurity, his fear of rejection, and his longing to be accepted by his fellows. He wants to be attractive and sophisticated. He may want to impress adults by appearing to be independent and mature. Advertising aimed at teenagers conveys subtle messages to them. Female desirability, or male attractiveness are communicated in messages in advertisements for such things as cosmetics, clothes, female underwear, motor-bikes and beer. The success of such advertising campaigns indicates how responsive vulnerable teenagers can be to these pressures.

Many teenagers find that advertising encourages them to spend more on clothes and cosmetics than they can really afford. Lack of money may add to the sense of frustration faced by a jobless teenager. As one stated: 'I'm geared to a life that makes me expect lots of things that only money can buy . . . and I haven't the money with which to buy these things . . . nor have I any hope of a job to get money to get these things. . . ' As a Christian family you will already have tackled the problems of life style, and hopefully your teenagers will not find that pressures from advertising pose major problems. It is unlikely that your child will remain uninfluenced by the media's subtle messages though be gentle with him if this is so, he is likely to be confused.

Job-hunting in a depressed market

If your teenager leaves school to join the dole queues of the 1980s (or even leaves university, with a degree, for the dole queue) then he is going to need much love and support. He will probably feel bitter, resentful, a failure and that life is purposeless. If you have brought him up to believe that God made man to work, and that man finds fulfilment in work, then he is going to question the character of a God who does not make sure there are enough jobs so that he can have just one chance in life. If you have taught him that it is good to work, and lazy and bad not to, then he will face inner turmoil. If he wants to listen, then you can try to explain to your jobless teenager that this state of affairs is not his fault. The baby boom of the 1960s produced a population explosion which is unlikely to work its way out of the system until the mid-1980s. It seems unlikely that the British economy will generate new jobs before then and so the problems of young jobless school leavers are unlikely to diminish before then. If he cannot find paid work then he may want to use his energy voluntarily helping the old, infirm or needy. At the very least he will feel that he is of use to someone and not totally useless in the world. His sense of values will be tested — especially for boys, as most men gain a sense of self-worth by the responsibility they are given at work. Loss of a job means diminishing self-worth to most men.

Use your initiative to help your teenager find work. Don't let him give up looking for work. Never let him feel that he is on the scrap-heap or that God has given him up. Show him that you love and accept him as God does but stear clear of pious cliches which will be meaningless to him at this stage.

Stand by your teenager in loyal support. Job hunting is a crucial and difficult task. Your teenager will face enormous emotional strain if he has been rejected time after time by prospective employers. His self-confidence suffers with each rejection and may even be totally lost, which makes it even harder for him to find that elusive, vital first job. Make sure that your teenager knows that you have confidence in him when he leaves school for college, for work, or to hunt for work. Your support will help him more than you realise.

15: Coming from a Christian home

Teenagers from Christian families react in different ways to their parents' Christianity: 'I've always been a Christian', one girl told me. Another admitted, 'I went through a stage of testing it all out for myself, but I've found my own faith now'. One man shared, 'My parents' religion seemed such a sham that I was put off God and all that for life. . . ' And from the child of a vicarage, 'I don't know why, but I totally oppose everything for which my parents stand . . . looking at me now, you'd never think my father was a vicar, would you?'

Your child and Christianity
Obviously you, as Christian parents, long for your children to find in Christianity all that you have found. You must, however, be prepared to be patient enough to let them discover Christ for themselves. They cannot inherit your faith along with their genetic make-up. Your child's faith must eventually be his own and not depend on you as its source and inspiration.

Many young people become Christians when they are teenagers. These are the years of idealism and of optimism. Young people are looking for worlds to conquer, and causes that are worth their life's commitment. They want their lives to be of value. Many find that Christianity does just this — sadly, many others find that it does not.

As your teenager is maturing be patient and prayerful about his faith, or lack of it. Make allowances for the fact that his present view of Christianity is coloured by the emotional changes taking place inside him, and that for a time his judgement may not be as clear as it will be later.

Because he reacts vigorously to everything, he will react to Christianity in an emotional way. He may want as little as possible to do with religion, and may long for you to leave him in peace to think things through quietly on his own. He may not want to be trundled off to church at Christmas, or on family occasions. He may resent it if you apply what he says is 'emotional black-mail' to get him there (this is about the only method you can use, as you cannot carry a kicking teenager into church!). If you push him too hard towards your religion then he may react by being the opposite of all you want. He may make a big drama of rejecting your faith. Alternatively he may retreat into a shell of resentment, and say little, but feel much.

If he does not want to go to church with you, then you may need to re-think your family church attendance. It is good to go together as husband and wife. But what of a teenager who is left alone every Sunday morning because the rest of the family is at church? He may join them out of loneliness and boredom, or he may resent the fact that the others attend church leaving him alone. I remember a Swiss woman who shared with me, 'In my teens I refused to go to church. Someone in my family always stayed in the house with me . . . I didn't know till later that this was carefully planned by them. They didn't want me to feel rejected, or out of things because I couldn't cope with church at that stage. The fact that one of them was always there at home with me meant that I always felt part of my family . . . and it was this that finally led me back to my parent's Christianity. One of them being there with me meant so much. . . '. Never push or shame your teenager into forced church attendance. Wait patiently and pray much. Go on believing that God, in his time and not yours, will bring your teenager to himself.

If you have a teenager who is rejecting your faith, then try to cut down on the number of evening meetings you attend to give him the time and love he craves from you. Help him to know that God is most important to you, that your marriage comes second, and that he (as one of your children) comes next. Remember that God may want you to be at home, rather than at meetings. In the end your child is more likely to come to God because of your love, and you will be glad you put him before meetings.

Your teenager has many things to sort out within himself as he thinks through Christianity. He may have inherited a whole cartload of hang-ups from you! He may have inherited taboos that make nonsense to him when he thinks about them. He may see in the out-workings of your faith little more than hypocrisy. Yet, as a Christian, the Holy Spirit lives within you: and despite all your deficiencies as a Christian and as a parent, trust the Holy Spirit to be seen in your life as your child watches you.

Your teenager may appear to reject your kind of Christianity, only to discover what you have found in a different form, which is valid to him. Accept him and his authenticity even if his faith does not seem to conform to yours. God has made us all differently and does not expect our relationships with him to be identical. Each is as unique as the individual concerned.

Avoid preaching to your teenager, and do not take him to evangelistic meetings if he is likely to feel resentful that he is being 'got at'. Be alert to any opportunities to introduce him to Christians with whom he may share interests as varied as music and mountaineering. Help him to meet Christians whose outlook on life is positive and joyful. Avoid those who are narrow and pietistic. Remember that God loves your child even more than you do, and he longs for your child to be his even more than you do. Trust God. Hang on to these facts through the lean years when faith, and rejection of faith, threatens to divide your family unless you can hold both sides together with love and tact.

Your teenager may question your beliefs about God. In a pluralistic society he may wonder why you claim that only one path leads to God. Your answers may only succeed in convincing him that the God you worship cannot be the God of love. He may veer towards universalism, as an alternative to having to believe that God would ever judge and punish. Superficial spirituality may lead him to seek a deeper spiritual life through Eastern religions. RE lessons at school may make your teenager question your beliefs about the Bible. Choose your words carefully when you answer him, so that definition of words does not cloud the real issue. Know where you stand on the authority of the Bible, and be ready to share this with your child.

Death and suffering

This is the time when your teenager is likely to face his first bereavement. It is at this stage that one, or all, of his grandparents are likely to die. The death of a grandparent is a major issue to children — complicated by the fact that the parent who is mourning the loss of a parent, may not notice that his child is also bereaved.

Allow your teenager to grieve when he faces bereavement. Do not encourage a stiff-upper-lip attitude. Do not stop him from venting anger at God if he needs to: 'God has killed my Gran!' is not really intended as blasphemy. God understands why your child may react like this. God is patient, loving and understanding of a teenager's grief.

It is usually helpful to allow your teenager to attend the funeral of a relative or of a friend. It is necessary for him, as for adults, to go through the rituals associated with bereavement, and to have the opportunity of formally saying goodbye to the one he has loved. If your teenager cannot express his grief at bereavement, and if he behaves peculiarly afterwards then seek skilled help for him.

Your teenager may question the nature of a God who allows suffering in his world. You may answer him with a long intellectual lecture on the problem of suffering. If you do this you probably will not be able to answer his deepest needs and questions, because he is asking from an emotional base and you are replying from a rational stance. Do your best, and trust that in time your teenager will accept that the God of love does not stop suffering in our world. Help your teenager to understand that the Christian response to suffering should be to do something to help to relieve it in others.

Points of conversion

Your teenager may be one of those who never experiences any real doubts about Christianity. He may go to church happily, and grow into a faith that is deep and real, which has never known any stages of crisis or of special decision for God. If this happens, then be grateful to God. However, remember that some teenagers feel rather like second-class citizens of the kingdom of heaven if they do not have an exciting conversion story to tell. One girl talked to me: 'I've always been a Christian. I can't remember a time when I wasn't. It doesn't sound like anything much though when I tell my friends that . . . they all have proper conversions that they talk about'. God's prime concern is that your children should be members of his kingdom, the means by which they enter his kingdom is of secondary importance. Help your teenager to grasp this fact.

If your teenager experiences a 'conversion' then be ready for major or minor disruption in the household. Any conversion changes a person, and an emotional teenager responds to his new found faith with an enthusiasm rather like falling in love for the first time. You will now understand why non-Christian parents say that their converted teenager has become a religious fanatic — you may even feel you have a fanatic in your own house! Do all you can to encourage your teenager to grow as a Christian. Rejoice with him in his new faith, rejoice in the way the Bible has come alive for him, and encourage him in his efforts at sharing his faith with others. If he is enthusiastically trying to 'convert' his brothers and sisters, or other relatives then try to teach him how to go about this without using a-bull-in-a-china-shop technique.

Encourage him in his new faith by your depth of spirituality. Help him to see that you study the Bible, and that you believe that prayer is so important that you spend time at this and give it priority over other things in your life. If this is in fact not the case then God may use your newly converted teenager to help you back to where God intends you to be as a Christian.

Do not squash your teenager's new found faith unless you have to. If he reads in the Bible 'Give all your goods to the poor. . .' and wants to give away his pocket money to refugees, and his used clothes to charity then try not to squash him in his obedience to what he believes God is telling him to do. Because he is a teenager he will tend to be over-enthusiastic in the way he lives out his Christianity. Wait, and in time his reactions will level off.

Fellowship at school
The school Christian Union may be important for development as a Christian. In it he will meet Christians of varying backgrounds and beliefs. He will meet Christians from different denominational backgrounds, which will be valuable for him. He will learn how to relate his Christianity to his school environment. With others at school he will share problems involved in being a Christian at school, how to face intellectual or ethical problems that may be posed through lessons, or through generally accepted attitudes and standards.

Some parents support their child's school by arranging a parent's prayer-meeting for the school and for the Christian Union. This is done with the Head's knowledge, and may occur several times a term. In this way concerned parents are able to pray together about the things that are important to them at that school — and one of those things will be the CU. Try though not to interfere with your teenager and his relationship with the school CU. If you are genuinely worried about something then tactfully talk to the member of staff responsible for the CU. Maintain a low profile, you cannot have the influence in a school CU that you have in your own church.

True friendships

Help your teenager to learn a balance between doing homework and attending Christian activities. Help him too to learn how to make friends with people outside his church circle, so that he is able to mix outside Christian circles and is someone God can use in the lives of those who never attend church. Do not encourage him to adopt a ghetto mentality, so that all his free time is spent in the company of fellow Christians, revolving round church activities. Make sure that he has healthy relationships with those outside the church, and that he learns to build friendships with all kinds of people. It is sad to see adult men and women who are unable to make friends with non-Christians because they have never learned to relate on a normal basis with people outside the church.

So encourage your Christian teenager to make friends with non-Christians. Help him to make real friendships and to learn to appreciate people as people — and not just as souls to be won for Christ. Help him to understand that in order to share his faith with a friend he must earn the right to speak, and that right is earned by true friendship (not by psuedo-friendship which has one aim in view only — to proselytise the so-called friend). If your teenager can learn this while he is young he will have learned lessons that are valuable to him in adult life.

Above all, your teenager needs to learn that relationships come first for Christians. Of prime importance is his relationships with God himself, then with his family and the church, and then with people outside the church.

Make sure that he knows that relationships are more important than clocking-up a certain number of attendances at meetings, and he will then view his faith with God's perspective.

16: Drink and drug abuse

Newspapers sometimes make uncomfortable reading for parents of teenagers. Headlines like: 'The teeny drunkards', 'One in seven youths has drink worry', and 'Crime wave by teenage alcoholics'. The usual reaction is: 'It couldn't happen in our family!' Yet figures show that it could happen in any family, and that you as the parents of teenagers need to take the current teenage drink problem very seriously.

Teenage alcoholism

A report in the *Daily Mail*, at the end of 1980 states: 'Most teenagers — even those who are only 14 — drink alcohol. Many of them get drunk. A growing number ruin their lives because drink becomes more important than their homes, their jobs and their friends.

'Home Office Minister, Timothy Raison, has appealed to the drinks' trade to help clamp down on teenage drunks.

'Yet our attitudes to the teenage alcohol crisis are wholly hypocritical. On the one hand we do everything to entice the most emotionally vulnerable members of our society into pubs. We provide flashing lights, throbbing music, space-invader machines and sophisticated looking cocktails which make the girls feel like Campari girls.

'Teenage boys with hardly a bristle to warrant a shave, are seduced by ads which imply that drinking beer with the lads will make them sexually potent. And then we fling up our hands in horror at the spectacle of drunken youth'.

The article continues: 'The director of the Leeds Council on Alcoholism said, "Of course all this makes me very angry — I have to deal with the results. Society is hypocritical. It laments the problem, but is not willing to provide the relatively small amount of money needed to prevent it. We need money to help educate youngsters in schools, to help them counter the very strong influences exerted on them that drinking is the grown-up, sophisticated thing to do" '.

The same article then points out, 'Alcohol is usually introduced to children by their parents, rather than by other children . . . the majority of youngsters are introduced to drink — "a proper glass, not a sip" — between the ages of 12–14, during some kind of family celebration'.

The Daily Telegraph in April 1981 claimed that 'one young man in every seven is now drinking at a level which will damage his health. . .'

The Observer had similarly grave words in 1981: 'Rising numbers of convicted teenagers are entering Britain's borstals as alcoholics and, a leading psychiatrist claims, an alarming number of people between the ages of 16 and 20 are committing crimes under the influence of drink'. This psychiatrist, Dr David Marjot, stated: 'There is not a distinctive social pattern amongst those we studied. They came from all strata of society. The present employment situation plays a part in the behaviour, but it is not entirely to blame. There are a number of factors such as copying parents or influenced by advertising. I think some control must be put on the amount of drink advertisements that children see. If they think that it is socially acceptable to drink then they will do so'.

The significance of alcohol

In the last twenty five years there has been a major increase in the production and distribution of alcohol throughout the world. The World Health Organisation now states that 'alcohol problems are a direct threat in many countries to social and economic progress'.

Did you know that about 90 per cent of adults in the United Kingdom drink alcohol at one time or another? Over 700,000 are estimated to be so dependent as to be classified as alcoholics. In the last twenty five years the amount of alcohol drunk in the UK has doubled. In 1980 the approximate amount of money spent in the UK on drink was £10,000 million. Over 700,000 people are employed full-time in the production and distribution of alcohol.

In recent years attitudes towards alcohol have changed. Drinking is now seen as a normal thing to do to relieve tension or anxiety. Alcohol is easier to buy than it used to be — in 1979 half the off-licenses in the UK were in supermarkets or grocer's shops, making alcohol easily accessible to shoppers, and to teenagers.

Statistics also confirm what you may have noticed: that since the war the age at which people start to drink has steadily fallen. The reason for this is not clear: some people attribute it to the insecurity of the present world, others to the pressures of competition, others to unemployment, and yet others to the changing nature of family life.

Alcohol abuse

In the report of a working party of the British Council of Churches, presented at the end of 1981, concern was expressed about alcohol and its abuse in today's society — concern which you, as a parent, dare not ignore. The report points out that alcohol is a depressant *drug*, which carries a risk of dependence. People who become heavily dependent on alcohol are called 'alcoholics'. But many people who are not dependent on alcohol *abuse* it. This becomes clearer when one definition of alcohol abuse is understood, it is, 'The consumption of alcohol to an extent that is harmful to oneself or to others'. Alcohol abuse occurs if the use of alcohol results in behaviour which does not respect others, or demeans oneself. This definition indicates that alcohol abuse is widespread. The report gives reasons why people drink to their own and other people's hurt: 'They do so to cope with stress; to relieve pain; to overcome loneliness; to stimulate appetite; to make friends; to defy other people; to symbolise spiritual or physical acts'. It continues, 'Much can be done to demonstrate that alcohol is not needed in order to be normal; to inculcate safe habits, especially among the young; and to offer the kind of support that can contribute to a person's regard for himself'.

The report goes on to comment that even light or moderate drinkers are at risk in unexpected ways — especially those who start drinking young, and who either have an alternative to alcohol or who reject alternatives. The working party would like to see society changing in its attitude towards alcohol; they believe that it should not be accepted that drinking is normal. They would like to see vulnerable individuals strengthened in their ability to resist alcohol, and want to see widespread realisation and acceptance of the dangers of excess.

Parental influence

The working party has a suggestion for adults — which applies to you, as parents: 'Avoid or carefully limit and control your drinking, both for your own sake and for the sake of the others you may influence — especially children'.

It is at this point that you as a Christian parent may feel bewildered. When you were a teenager yourself alcohol was probably not drunk in your home, especially if you come from an evangelical Christian background. It was taboo twenty years ago for evangelical Christians to smoke, drink or dance. The Christian life tended to be full of negative prohibitions. In the last two decades Christian attitudes have tended to change. From a narrow piety that was full of 'Thou shalt not' attitudes, regarded as vital for a 'victorious' Christian life, a more positive life style has been generally adopted. Many activities that used to be regarded as 'worldly' in the past, are now seen as good gifts from a Creator God given for his children's enjoyment. Alcohol has come into this category for some Christians: formerly they would never have drunk alcohol but now they enjoy it.

You may be among those who now enjoy alcohol as one of the gifts God has given you. If this is so, then think carefully and prayerfully about what is now happening in society around you. Are your teenagers facing the risk of being introduced to alohol by you, of accepting alcohol as normal for anyone, and of imperceptibly slipping into drinking in excess? If you give your child his first drink, then you must accept part of the blame for any problems later on.

The remedy

You will find no easy answer to the teenage drink problem. Christian parents differ on what they believe should be done. There are those who assert that teenagers must be taught how to handle alcohol for themselves, so that as adults they know how to drink within strict self-imposed control. If you come into this category then remember that you face having to handle your teenager when he is drunk — since he will probably experiment at some time or other to see what it is like to get drunk. If he lurches home drunk, and you bundle him to bed with little sympathy, and make him get up and go to school or work the next day rather than indulge his hang-over in bed, then he will have learned how dreadful it feels the day after. This experience may be sufficient to stop him from drinking in excess again. However, if your teenager drinks, you can never be absolutely sure that he is not growing dependent on alcohol. If he turns to the bottle for comfort in stress, loneliness or unhappiness then he is learning a pattern of behaviour that will not help him as an adult. He is running away from painful, situations and escaping into drugged unreality.

This is where Christianity has a positive contribution to make. Not in a negative 'Thou shalt not drink' attitude; but rather in helping to bring healing to the hurts that can lead to alcohol abuse. With the redemption that Christ offers, comes forgiveness and personal acceptance both by God and by the church. Above all the Holy Spirit (living in those who come to God, and accept him as Saviour and Lord) is the agent for change in a life. Knowing that God loves and cares for him, can enable an individual to face stress and sorrow creatively, rather than destructively reaching for the bottle to anaesthetise grief and to blot out problems.

Giving up drink

You may find it better to stop drinking yourselves, even though you may have recently found that God has given you the liberty to enjoy drink in moderation among the many good things he has given mankind. As parents you may decide, for the sake of your children, that you should stop having any alcohol, so that they will never see alcohol consumption as a normal pattern in their family life, which they will copy in their own adult lives. If there is no alcohol in the house then there is none for your teenager to drink (free of charge). You may later be glad that you adopted this attitude of not using your liberty to cause another to stumble — especially if you sense that any one of your teenagers is a potential alcohol abuser.

You will need to find alternative drinks if you are going to give up alcohol. Learn how to make non-alcoholic punches for parties and festive occasions. These can be very good. Build traditions in your family for celebrations that do not require alcohol as part of the celebration.

If you have given up drinking then do not feel ashamed or embarrassed about this. The blushing embarrassed Christian at a party apologetically asking for orange juice or the Christian who turns his wine glass rudely upside down at a dinner party, can make things awkward for others. Don't be apologetic if you have decided not to drink, and don't behave in such a way that others feel you are condemning them. Your stand will usually be respected but make it unobtrusively and with no awkwardness. Do your homework, and find out the kind of alternatives to alcohol that are available at the parties and dinners you usually attend, so that you know what to ask for.

The drug scene

The popularity of drug abuse varies from time to time, according to what is available or fashionable. At one extreme are teenagers who indulge in glue-sniffing, and at the other are those who inject a morphine derivative into their veins. Your children are not automatically immune from the dangers of drug abuse: they are human and may experiment like other children and become hooked as other teenagers may. Try to help them to understand the dangers of drug abuse, without dramatising it in such a way that they will want to experiment — or they may use drugs just to express independence of you.

Today's world tends to be a drug-centred culture. Drugs like alcohol, aspirin and nicotine are almost universally accepted. Your child will be influenced by his friends: if they use a certain drug then he is likely to try it too. One interesting study in the United States revealed that nine out of ten teenagers who had never used any mind-altering drugs (such as marijuana, cocaine and alcohol) felt that they had a very close relationship with their parents. Those who used drugs did not feel this way about their parents. In this study, the non-users tended to be among the brightest academically and were also involved in extra-curricular activities at school. Eighty per cent stated that religion was important to them. Eight out of ten said that their parents tended to check on their whereabouts, and to know where they were and who they were with most of the time. They also considered themselves to be more independent than their classmates, and claimed that their non-use of drugs or alcohol had little to do with fear of arrest or of parental disapproval. Those who were well adjusted, busy at school and church saw no necessity to drink or to use drugs. They possessed sufficient self-esteem to stand out and to be different from the crowd.

Getting help

If you think that your child may be drinking too much or may be involved in the drug scene, then take sensible precautions. Lock up your money, so that he cannot steal from your wallet or purse — he will do so if he needs drink or drugs. Lock up, or throw away all possible addictive drugs your doctor may have prescribed to you in the past — this includes valium, mogadon, and anti-depressant medicines as well as more obvious barbiturates.

Try to find out why your child may be reacting in this way. What is lacking in his life that has led him in this direction? Is it his social contacts, his friends, or his love life? Why has he escaped into a world of drugs? Someone outside the family will probably be able to help more than you can. Do seek help sooner rather than later.

This is likely to be a problem that you will not be able to handle on your own; in fact, parents tend to adopt attitudes towards an alcoholic or addicted child that may be the opposite of what that child most needs. So, seek help for yourselves as soon as possible as parents, and for your child once he realises that he needs help. Remember that stress between parents can drive a teenager to escape the tension at home through drink or drugs. Alcoholics Anonymous has support groups for the relatives of alcoholics, from which you can learn much that you will need to know and understand.

If your child faces a drink or drug problem then do not hide away in shame. You need help as a family and must not be too afraid or too ashamed to seek professional help. Your child's future hangs on this.

In a society where alcoholism is a growing teenage problem never complacently assume, 'It can't happen to us'. It can!

17: When to seek help

Almost all teenagers eventually have to come to terms with aspects of themselves that they dislike. Most of these things have to be accepted as an inevitable part of that teenager's life but some areas can be changed, and some can be helped greatly by correct medical treatment.

Physical problems

Your teenager does not have to suffer the permanent embarrassment of severe acne — blackheads which become infected, and are not only unsightly but also may cause permanent scars on the face. Many of the simple remedies in your chemist's shop, which you can buy over the counter are effective, and well worth trying. Make sure that your teenager washes his hair frequently with an anti-dandruff shampoo if he has acne, as this may help him. Make sure that he is getting sufficient sleep and that his life is not excessively stressful. Lack of sleep, and tension, can make acne worse. The stress of exams or the stress of pre-menstrual tension are other possible factors in the occurrence of acne.

If home remedies do not work and your teenager is embarrassed about his acne then encourage him to go to his doctor. Modern treatment is able to help, but only your own doctor knows whether your child is a suitable candidate for certain forms of treatment or not, or if it is best to leave the acne to settle on its own with the passing of the years.

If your daughter experiences severe pains with her periods then encourage her to go to her doctor for help. It should not be necessary for her to be off school or off work at this time of the month, if she receives adequate help. Don't panic if the help given entails her being put on a contraceptive pill regularly. This is not a license for promiscuity — it is a recognised way of treating menstrual pain with the hormones contained in the pill. If your daughter has excessively heavy periods then make sure that she isn't getting anaemic — your doctor's help is again needed in this.

Warning signs
There are certain signals that should alert you to seek professional help with your teenager. Obviously he needs professional help if he runs away from home often; if he is in trouble with the law; if he skips school regularly; or if he is a heavy drug user.

Other signals that should alert you to the possibility that all is not well include a sudden withdrawal from people, dropping his friends, and the sense that he is isolated in a private world of his own. These signs may herald the onset of depression which is faily common in teenagers. If he talks of suicide then regard this as a red flag signalling for help. Don't take a suicide threat lightly — suicide is second only to accidents as the cause of teenage deaths. If your teenager talks of killing himself then get help immediately from a professionally qualified person. As teenagers are impulsive creatures, protect them from the impulses that can be destructive, and lock up all medicines all the time. Teenage depression is common, and can be treated successfully medically, so don't hesitate to go to your own doctor for help.

If your teenager faces a bereavement when he is emotionally disturbed then be tactful and patient with him. His emotional disturbance may make him feel that everything is unreal. He may almost feel as if he is standing apart from himself, in the audience, like watching himself act on a stage. This is a protective mechanism of the mind, to prevent him from feeling too intensely when he cannot cope with deep feelings. After the death of a loved one your teenager may appear indifferent, and

156

show no obvious signs of grief. Recognise this as a protective armour and the result of emotional numbness; do not assume your teenager is callous — far from it! Do not break down this natural barrier without providing adequate help, and since most parents are not trained to do this it is usually best left to a professional. Make sure that your teenager knows that you love him at the time of grief. He needs the assurance of your love. Help him to know that you are standing by him. He will be more bewildered than you are, as to why he is not feeling the grief that he knows he should. He will long to be able to share his bewilderment with someone who understands the reasons lying deep within himself that he himself cannot understand. If he talks to you about it, then don't force his confidence, or pry into his thoughts. If you do this then he may flee back into his protective shell again. If your teenager needs help then your doctor or your pastor should be able to arrange it for you.

Slimming and starving

Teenagers are naturally self-critical, and this self-criticism can lead to a dangerous possibility. At the age of about fourteen your daughter may begin to criticise her shape. 'I'm going on a slimming diet', she may well announce. You probably heave a sigh of relief: you had not liked to tell her bluntly but she was getting far too podgy. At first you probably encourage her to slim, and both of you are pleased with the resulting trim figure that emerges from the puppy-fat.

Do be careful about this. Some girls carry slimming to an extreme — and may even make themselves vomit any food they have eaten. If this goes on for long enough then your daughter's periods may stop, and her emaciated body indicates her desire not to appear feminine. Her rejection of food is believed to be a totally unconscious desire to stay in a sexless shape, with undeveloped breasts like a child. If things reach this stage then your daughter will probably need to be admitted to hospital for treatment. She is seriously ill — ill enough possibly to die without adequate treatment.

Anorexia nervosa

Once your teenager is being treated for *anorexia nervosa* you may find that you have to face the shattering fact that medical opinion may hold you responsible for your teenager's illness. It is now thought that the hormone changes which cause periods to stop in anorexia nervosa occur as a result of the illness rather than being the cause of it. The cause is at a psychological level rather than hormonal. Some specialists believe that the root cause lies within the anorexic's family: and especially if there are problems in communication between mother and daughter. It has been claimed that the parents of anorexics seem unable to give their teenagers the confidence they need. If you have difficulty in talking openly about sex to your teenager then this may pose a problem for her, causing sex to appear frightening and something that she does not understand. She may not want to grow up into a world where she is an adult woman. She does not know why she starves herself, and this is done from an unconscious motive. However, in starving herself she is clinging onto childhood, and avoiding reaching full womanhood. When her periods stop (as they will) she may feel less threatened.

Some mothers of anorexic girls become very domineering. Even the worry of their daughter's illness alone can make a mother more dominant than she would otherwise be. It has been noticed in one hospital that after parents visit their anorexic daughter in hospital that the daughter's weight is likely to drop. This may be because her parents are the people who matter most in an anorexic teenager's life: their visit may upset her enough to make her lose weight again. Sometimes both daughter and parents with, or without knowing it, want to remain dependent on one another. If your daughter has this illness then it will be up to you to take the initiative, and to help your daughter face impending adult life without close ties to you as is normally the case.

If your daughter has this illness then it is possible that you will feel guilty, that you have failed as a parent. It is no good blaming yourself for what is past. Your daughter is ill and needs help: and she will be helped more by your strength rather than by you indulging in guilt. However, it is possible that you yourself will need professional help yourself to enable you to do this. Go to your doctor and get a clear explanation from him as to why your daughter is as she is. If necessary ask him for medicines to help you handle yourself until your emotions have stabilised. You may also want to talk to your minister about any feelings of guilt and failure. It is therapeutic to share this burden with another person, and together to realise the liberating fact that God has accepted and forgiven you: and with his forgiveness he receives you unconditionally.

Doing your best

There are few parents who do not face apparent failure as parents of teenagers at some stage or other. And I expect that you, like me, feel from time to time that you have failed your children. Had you known more, you might have acted differently. You did what you thought was best at the time but experience proves that what you did was wrong. It is now too late to put that wrong right.

As a Christian parent you must accept that God's forgiveness and love embraces even your failures at parenting. He knew, when he first entrusted you with your children, that you would handle them as you have. Your children will suffer the consequences of your mishandling but God, in his grace, transmutes dross into gold. Your mistakes in your child's life can be used by God to produce a personality of special sensitivity and special understanding. In God's hands even mistakes can be turned into something good and beautiful — and this is never more evident that in the lives of our children.

God does not call us to be perfect parents but he does

intend us to be the best that we can be. He intends us to utilise our full potential both as people and as parents. Do your best, work at being the best parent you are capable of being, and then leave the rest to God. In his capable hands your children are safe.